Fish TALES

A COLLECTION OF ANGLING STORIES

A Fisherman's Petition

O, Ananias! Father of all lies,
Inspire me here beneath these summer skies,
While I recline among mendacious guys,
That I, too, may depict the phantom rise
Of that 'lost fish' of most enormous size.
Give me the patience to sit calmly by,
While amateurs with veterans gravely vie
Recounting deeds performed with rod and fly,
Then help me tell the final, crowning lie!

Anon

Fish TALES

A COLLECTION OF ANGLING STORIES

EDITED BY *Tom Quinn*

ALAN SUTTON

First published in the United Kingdom in 1992 by
Alan Sutton Publishing Limited
Phoenix Mill · Far Thrupp · Stroud · Gloucestershire

First published in the United States of America in 1992 by
Alan Sutton Publishing Inc · Wolfeboro Falls · NH 03896–0848

British Library Cataloguing in Publication Data

Fish Tales: A Collection of Angling Stories
I. Quinn, Tom
799.1

ISBN 0–7509–0091–1

Library of Congress Cataloging in Publication Data applied for

Cover illustration: Missed by a Head *by A. Rowland Knight*

Typeset in 10/13 Garamond.
Typesetting and origination by
Alan Sutton Publishing Limited.
Printed in Great Britain by
The Bath Press, Bath, Avon.

Contents

Fish Tales

Fish Tales

Fish Tales

Acknowledgements

For their help with suggestions, contributions and the loan of rare books I would like to thank Mary Corbett, Sandy Leventon, Laraine Plummer, Toby Buchan, Badger Walker, Barbara O'Flaherty, Debbie Fischer, Chris Greenhough and the staff of the British Library.

Introduction

Fishing with rod and line has probably inspired more literary endeavour than any other sport. Why this should be is something of a mystery, but since the mid-seventeenth century, when Isaac Walton's *Compleat Angler* first appeared, fishermen have struggled with pen and paper to explain their reasons for pursuing a sport that ordinary mortals find at best dull and at worst absurd.

Certainly angling attracts those of a literary cast of mind, and it is a mistake to think that all angling books are written by fishermen for fishermen. Books of the practical, how-to-do-it variety fit this category, but many others attempt to do far more; they attempt to reproduce on the printed page the exact atmosphere of a day's fishing, in order perhaps to woo a wider audience with the excitement and poetry of the thing. And it is the best and most enduring of these attempts that I have collected here.

One or two readers may be disappointed that some of the best-known fish stories do not appear. There is nothing for example from Hemingway's *The Old Man and the Sea*, but since the story, though undeniably great, has little to do with angling, I felt justified in leaving it out. And there is nothing from *The Compleat Angler* simply because, although it is certainly one of the greatest of all attempts to describe the pleasures of fishing, it is already extraordinarily well known – after the Bible, it is the world's most reprinted book. Other oft-reprinted stories do not appear simply because I thought it was time to let some of the great, but long forgotten, voices of the past have their say instead. I have therefore concentrated, though not exclusively, on what many consider to be the heydey of angling writing, the years 1880–1910.

These were the years when the railways had newly opened up the country and some of its best fishing to intelligent, literate men who were paying increasing attention to fishing tackle and techniques, and to the scientific study of the fish themselves. The turn of the century was also a time when industry

Isaac Walton: 'literary inspiration'

was still concentrated in a few centres and much of the rest of the country was untouched by chemical and industrial pollution. Most of our rivers were therefore still sparkling clean, and vast numbers of new towns and suburbs had not yet led to the horrors of abstraction and dredging.

Better still (though one says this with trepidation!) there were fewer anglers, and the pressure on a delicate resource was therefore that much less. In short then, the years 1880–1910 are something of a golden age; an age of glorious fishing that is never likely to return. But the pleasures of that unsullied time were captured, like insects in amber, in the myriad fishing books published over those years.

I have also been shamelessly arbitrary in my selection of material. Thus one or two of my favourite writers are heavily represented – J.H.R. Bazeley and

H.T. Sheringham for example – but I would justify this on the grounds that their work has been unavailable for too long and there is simply a great deal of it that is very good.

Some extracts have been included because they come as close as we are ever likely to get to the reason we fish; others because they are beautifully written; yet others because they bring to life again battles with great or record fish.

In recent years there has been a tendency to increasing specialization among anglers, and it is rare for a fisherman to pursue game, coarse and sea fish, or even to take much of an interest in branches of the sport other than his own. This is a sad development because the distinction between coarse and game (or sea for that matter) is an entirely modern and arbitrary one. Ideas of the superiority of one branch of the sport over another are also untenable in an historical context. Salmon fishing, for example, may now seem to be the most aristocratic form of the sport, but at the end of the nineteenth century pike fishing was generally much more in demand and therefore more expensive. It is only fashion, the increasing rarity of the salmon and the relative abundance of the pike that has led to the present situation.

I have not split the book into sections covering coarse, game and sea, because I wanted the three types of fishing to appear together, as they should, in one book: there is no reason why the salmon fisherman should not enjoy accounts, of, for example, a magnificent bass caught from the surf, or why the sea angler should not enjoy stirring tales of giant carp taken from deep, lily-covered ponds.

Whatever your interest in fishing I hope you will find much here to enjoy. And though it may be true that angling literature is a backwater compared with the great movements in English and world literature, it is nonetheless a fascinating one, full of twists and turns, full indeed of the pleasures of fishing itself.

The Salmon Fisher and His Wife

*A*nglers are nothing if not superstitious, but superstition can be taken to absurd extremes, as this fascinating – if rather sexist! – extract from one of the best-loved salmon fishing writers of the past reveals.

But one superstition lingers still, and lingers in spite of the fact that many ladies angle for love of the sport and that their luck is most excellent – indeed does not Miss Ballantine hold the record for a salmon taken on rod and line in these islands? But I had never, till the other day, known that it is an atavism of the angler that a man should be so ready to be accompanied by his wife and he going to the river. I had thought that he wanted her society, even her services with tea-kettles and so on. And that if he spoke crossly to her or was over-critical of her tea-making or her mulling of a hot drink, it was just because he felt that way. And then I read in an old print – the *Dundee Advertiser* of sixty years since – as follows:

A salmon-fisher was brought to the police court for continual illtreatment of his wife; this he admitted but he explained that it was done not for ill-will toward her but to attract salmon. This superstition has its counterpart in other lands than our own where the woman is looked upon as a sinister influence affecting the fish and fishing questions and the quantities of fish that are caught.

F i s h   T a l e s

So now you understand. And when you next hear Edwin (with a Durham Ranger in his cap) tell Angelina (and the tears in her pretty blue eyes) that her hut tea is a damnable dish wash and that she herself is vermin, you may be sure (when he stamps out of the hut lighting his pipe and leaving his lady to rinse the cups and ready the table) that he will catch a thirty pounder as soon as his fly is in the river.

Patrick Chalmers, *Where the Spring Salmon Run,* 1931.

There is an idea that game fishermen are always and necessarily gentlemen. The following extract reveals that things are occasionally quite otherwise. . . .

It was not a little provoking, after exhausting all my skill and patience for such a length of time and with so little success, to look over the bridge, and see the bed of the river where I had been fishing absolutely black with grilse. I could only comfort myself with the reflection that others seemed to succeed no better.

Lawless partly accounted for my bad sport by the fact of so many having fished the water before me; and I accordingly resolved, by his advice, to commence the attack very early the next morning. He promised to call me before daylight, but, awaking about three o'clock, I got up before he came, and walked down to the riverside, which I reached just as day was breaking.

How great then was my disappointment to perceive, through the morning's haze, an angler already fishing on that very wall, which I had expected to have all to myself for at least an hour or two! But infinitely was my surprise and displeasure increased when, upon approaching, I discovered that the person who had thus balked my sport was the identical Mr Lawless! who, thinking me very safe in bed until he chose to call me, had very carefully fished over the water race and killed a salmon; and was then engaged in fishing it the second time, after which he intended to wake me, as he thought, without giving a single hint of his morning's employment.

I was indeed provoked to think that the man who was eating my bread and salt should thus be the one to mar my amusement; and my feelings were even hurt at such an instance of treachery on the part of a brother sportsman. I shall not easily forget his face on first seeing me. I not only afterwards exposed him to some whose good opinion was of consequence to him, but think that I also succeeded in making him ashamed of himself before we parted.

Anon, *The Angler in Ireland, 1820.*

Fishing with Halford

That great exponent of nymph fishing, G.E.M. Skues here describes a meeting with Frederic Halford, perhaps the greatest exponent of the dry fly. If there is an edge to Skues' tone I think we can be sure that, given each man's devotion to his chosen technique, it was entirely intentional!

We had heard on the day of our arrival in Winchester that the great man was putting up at The George and was nightly welcoming his worshippers at that hotel to hear him expound the pure and authentic gospel of the dry fly – which no one would dream of questioning. So that evening found us, after our meal, among the humble listeners. It came to our ears on that occasion that we were to have the great man's company on the Abbots Barton water, the lessee having invited him for a week.

With becoming reverence we listened to his words of wisdom until it became necessary that the session be broken up. On the following day we were on the water a quarter of an hour or so before our mentor's arrival – taking the side stream, my friend above in the Ducks' Nest Spinney, I a couple of hundred yards further downstream, thus leaving the main river, the fishing of which was reputed the better, to the great man. He was not long behind us and presently we saw him casting on Winnel Water, the main river. Soon afterwards he crossed the meadow which divided the two streams and accosted me from the left bank of the side stream to advise us kindly on the fly to put up, and to make his advice clearer he cast his fly on the right bank of the side stream, having first ascertained that I had mounted a fly of George Holland's dressing, known as the quill marryat. He insisted that his fly, which was an india-rubber olive, was the right fly. My selection was based on little pale duns seen on the water. I took a look at his fly and was not a little shocked to see how coarse was the gut on which his fly was tied, but I was also too polite or timid to venture on such a comment.

We met at lunch-time and he inquired how I had done. I said two and a half brace. He had one trout only, but congratulated me civilly and offered to put me up for the Flyfishers' Club, then recently formed. Not expecting, despite my additional thirteen pounds in ten days, to live long enough to make it worthwhile, I declined and did not in fact seek membership till the autumn of 1893, when a voyage to the Cape and back had gone a long way to re-establishing my health.

Halford only fished the Abbots Barton length for three more days of his week, but just as I had been profoundly shocked to do better than the great master did on the first day, I was fated to be similarly shocked on each of his three other days. Yet it encouraged me to rely most on my own observations and not to attach undue importance to authority. My friend, by the way, caught the biggest fish of the week (one pound thirteen ounces), but it was his only catch.

G.E.M. Skues, *Itchen Memories,* 1931.

Fish Tales

Trout of a Lifetime

J.W. Hills' A Summer on the Test, first published in 1924, is a book that many of us are more than happy to return to again and again, and no book of great angling tales would be complete without an extract from it. What follows is Hills' beautiful description of how he caught his best ever trout on a floating fly.

Those who fish rivers where mayfly come will agree that, though with it you get a higher average weight, yet actually the biggest fish are killed on the sedge. 1903 on the Kennet was a great mayfly season for heavy fish, and a friend of mine who had the Ramsbury water got the truly remarkable bag of six fish in one day which weighed over nineteen pounds: and yet the two heaviest fish of the year were got on the sedge. I got the heaviest. It was the 26 July, a cloudy, gusty day, with a downstream wind, and I was on the water from eleven till five without seeing a rise. My friend and I then had tea and walked up the river at a quarter past six. Olives began to appear and trout to move; and suddenly a really large one started rising. We stood and watched, with growing excitement. He was taking every fly, in solid and determined fashion, and the oftener he appeared the bigger he looked, and the faster beat our hearts. It was settled that I was to try for him. I was nervous and uncomfortable. He was very big: it was a long throw and the wind horrible: I could not reach him, and like a fool I got rattled and pulled off too much line: there was an agonised groan from my friend behind me when a great curl of it was slapped on the water exactly over the trout's nose. We looked at each other without speaking, and he silently walked away up the river, leaving me staring stupidly at the spot where the trout had been rising. Of course he was gone.

The next two hours can be passed over. The small fly rise came and went. I caught a trout on a No. 2 silver sedge and finally, at about a quarter past eight, found myself gazing gloomily at the place where I had bungled. The wild wind had blown itself out and had swept the sky bare of cloud. Silence had come, and stillness. The willows, which all through the long summer day had bowed and chattered in the wind, were straightened and motionless, each individual leaf hanging down as though carved in jade: the forest of great sedges, which the gusts had swept into wave after wave of a roaring sea of emerald, was now calm and level, each stalk standing straight and stiff as on a Japanese screen. There

Trout leaping. A scraperboard illustration by Denys Watkins Pitchford, author of *The Confessions of a Carp Fisher*

had occurred that transition, that transmutation from noise and movement to silence and peace, which would be more wonderful were we not so accustomed to it, when a windy summer day turns over to a moveless summer night: when the swing and clatter and rush of the day is arrested and lifted from the world, and you get the sense that the great hollow of the air is filled with stillness and quiet, as with a tangible presence.

They are peaceful things, these summer evenings after wild days, and I remember particularly that this was one of the most peaceful; more so indeed than my thoughts, which were still in a turmoil. I stood watching mechanically, and then, tempting fate to help me, made a cast or two over the spot where the fish had been. How easy it was to reach it now, how lightly my fly settled on the water, how gracefully it swung over the place. All to no purpose, of course, for nothing happened, and I was about to reel up when a fish rose ten yards above, close under my bank. It was one of those small movements difficult to place. It might be a very large fish or a very small one. A wild thought swept through me that this was my big one: but no, I said to myself, it cannot be. This is not where he was rising. Besides, things do not happen like that, except in books: it is only in books that you make a fearful bungle and go back later and see a small break which you think is a dace, and cast carelessly and hook something the size of an autumn salmon: it is only in books that fate works in such fashion. Why, I know it all so well that I could write it out by heart, every move of it. But this is myself by a river, not reading in a chair. This is the real world, where such things do not happen: that is the rise of a half-pound trout.

I cast. I was looking right into the west, and the water was coloured like skimmed milk by reflection from where the sun had set. My silver sedge was as visible as by day. It floated down, there was a rise, I struck, and something rushed upstream. Then I knew. Above me was open water for some twenty-five yards, and above that again a solid block of weed, stretching right across. My fish made for this, by short, irresistible runs. To let him get into it would have been folly: he must be stopped: either he is well hooked or lightly, the gut is either sound or rotten: kill or cure, he must be turned, if turned he can be: so I pulled hard, and fortunately got his head round and led him down. He played deep and heavy and I had to handle him roughly, but I brought him down with a smash, and I began to breathe again. But then another terror appeared. In the place we had reached the only clear water was a channel under my bank, and the rest of the river was choked with weed.

Should I try to pull him down this channel, about three or four yards wide, to the open water below? No. It was much too dangerous, for the fish was uncontrollable, and if he really wanted to get to weed he would either get there or break me: even with a beaten fish it would be extremely risky, and with an unbeaten one it was unthinkable. Well, if he would not come down he must go up, and up he went willingly enough, for when I released pressure he made a long rush up to the higher weed bed, whilst I ran up the meadow after him, and with even greater difficulty turned him once more. This time I thought he was really going right through it, so fast and so heavy was his pull, and I think he was making for a hatch hole above: but once more my gallant gut stood the strain and, resisting vigorously, he was led down again. This proceeding was repeated either two or three times more, I forget which: either three or four times we fought up and down that twenty-five yards of river.

By then he was tiring, and I took up my station in the middle of the stretch, where I hoped to bring him in: my hand was actually on the sling of the net when he suddenly awoke and rushed up. He reached the weed bed at a pace at which it was impossible to stop, shot into it like a torpedo, and I had the sickening certainty that I should lose him after all. To hold him hard now would be to make a smash certain, so I slacked off: when he stopped I tightened again, expecting miserably to feel the dead, lifeless drag of a weeded line. Instead, to my delight, I found I was still in contact with the fish, and he was pulling hard. How he had carried the line through the weeds I do not know. To look at it seemed impossible . . . But the line was clear, and the fish proved it by careering wildly on towards the hatch, making the reel sing. I believe he meant to go through into the carrier, as fish have done before and after, but I turned him. However, we could not stay where we were.

The hatch was open at the bottom, there was a strong draw of water through it, and if a heavy, beaten fish got into this, no gut would hold him up. At all risks he must be taken over the weed into the clear water. I pulled him up to the top and ran him down. Then, for the first time after so many perils, came the conviction that I should land him. He was obviously big, but how big could not be known, for I had not had a clear sight of him yet. He still pulled with that immovable, quivering solidity only shown by a very heavy fish. But at last even his great strength tired. He gave a wobble or two, yielded and suddenly he was splashing on the top, looking huge in the dusk.

There ensued that agonising time when you have a big fish nearly beat, but he is still too heavy to pull in, and nothing you can do gets him up to the net. At last I pulled him over to it, but I lifted too soon, the ring caught in the middle of the body, he wavered a moment in the air and then toppled back into the water with a sickening splash. A judgment, I thought, and for a shattering second I believed he had broken the gut, but he was still on. I was pretty well rattled by then and, in the half light, made two more bad shots, but the end came at last, he was in the net and on the bank.

How big was he? Three pounds? Yes, and more. Four pounds? Yes, and more. Five? He might be, he might. My knees shook and my fingers trembled as I got him on the hook of the steelyard. He weighed a fraction over four pounds eight ounces.

J.W. Hills, *A Summer on the Test, 1924.*

A Record Pike

Alfred Jardine, a much-loved Victorian writer and fisherman, long held the British pike record. Here is his account of the capture of that mighty fish.

On 4 September 1879, I fished a little lake of fifteen acres in Buckinghamshire. The weather was very stormy and tempestuous. My punt was rather small and shallow; and the gale increasing, it was dangerous to keep out in the middle of the lake exposed to the full force of the wind. I therefore shifted to the leeward side of an island, where in ten feet of water I expected to find a monster pike, which some months previously had smashed up the rod and tackle of a brother angler, who was then fishing with me. I baited with a half-pound dace and cast it into the open channel between some weeds. I waited but a short while before I had a run, and drove my snap tackle well home. The pike immediately made a mad rush, taking nearly a hundred yards of line off my reel, and leaped some feet out of the water; this was several times repeated, but my salmon gut trace held firm. I had the pike well in hand, and in twenty minutes it was gaffed and safe in my punt.

The fish measured forty-seven inches in length, twenty-five inches girth; and that afternoon, in the presence of Mr W.H. Brougham, late secretary of the Thames Angling Preservation Society, weighed thirty-seven pounds. This pike was probably induced by the tempestuous weather to feed fearlessly, and thus lost its life. It and another of thirty-six pounds (both set up in the same glass case) adorn my collection of specimen fish.

Some winters ago, I fished the Frome with the late Mr J.P. Wheeldon, when the quieter parts of the river and its backwaters were frozen over, but in the main channel thick slabs of ice were hurrying along the swift-flowing current towards Poole Harbour. We fished close up to the land-locked ice, and our floats would again and again disappear under the edge of it, as, hungered into madness, some plunging pike seized our live baits, perhaps to rush out among the ice-floes, when it required all our skill to play and secure the fish. At other times, our lines would be severed by the sharp edges of the ice, and the fish escaped; but we had grand sport, and killed many big fish in spite of the bitter weather. My friend graphically described our experiences in *The Sportsman* of 10 January 1894.

In a far-off western county, as Jardine and I conned over each day's fishing, Death stalked rampant with such mercilessly cruel grip in his strong bony hands and throttling fingers as choked and crushed the warm breath of life from man's weak frame, as also in countless numbers and instances from the hardier birds and wild animals which could not live and exist with no better shelter than the open woods and bleak fields could supply.

Two tramps were found locked together in one another's arms for warmth, yet frozen to death in the cruel snow. Rabbits and partridges were stumbled upon, stiff and hard under the leaves and tussocks of dead grass. Birds in great numbers dropped dead from their roosting places in the trees, while living creatures were so utterly worn out and starved from the effects of relentless cold and want of food, that I positively caught starlings with my hands, too weak to fly away from bushes by the roadside; and almost set my clutch upon live rabbits, who only just managed to scuttle away from dry nooks under sheltered thorn bushes across the depths of frostcrisped snow-drifts, too deep to follow them without plunging in up to one's middle. The very men who rowed our boats each day (and we had each morning to break it out from thick ice, the result of a single night's frost) fairly shirked their job; and yet they were hardy shore-fishermen and deep-sea dredgers, accustomed to bear the brunt of the very worst wintry weather bowling round the neighbouring coast. Said one of them to me as he was loosing the ice round the boat one bitterly cold morning, 'I wonders how you soft-'anded Lunnon folks stands it.' I wondered too; and yet we did, day after day, in the teeth

of such ironlike frosts and blinding snow-storms as I would not again face –
no – not for a whole boat-load of twenty-pounders. Jardine put me up to a
little dodge, and a very good one it is in frosty weather, of wrapping thick
pledgets of cotton-wool, thoroughly saturated with castor-oil, round the
inner and outer sides of the rings of the rod, fastening them in their places
with whippings of fine thread. This certainly held the frost in check, and
enabled us to fish fairly comfortably, although every now and then the line
got absolutely clogged with big beads of ice, which prevented it running
freely through the rings. Beyond that we suffered little or no unpleasantness,
for the sport being simply magnificent and the fish feeding very quickly,
that alone kept us at fever-heat; and I think that on the whole we stood the
cold even a shade better than either of the boatmen did.

It was certainly terrible hard work for them; for the oars, from the broad
blades right away up to the very handles, were a solid mass of ice as thick as
a man's thigh; and this extra weight alone, combined with constantly holding the heavy lumbering craft steady, in the set of a strong stream, as first
one and then the other angler was busily employed in steering a powerful
fish from dangerous quarters under great drifts and floes of floating ice,
made an occasional stoppage for the sake of warming a pannikin of strong
coffee over a spirit lamp, and adding thereto a good swig of old brandy, an
uncommonly welcome relief to the crew all round.

Alfred Jardine, *Pike and Perch*, 1898.

A Very High Victorian

Most anglers who had the advantage and pleasure of Francis Francis's friendship
will remember how that past master of the gentle art hated to be bored and
interfered with while he was fishing, especially by anyone who knew little or
nothing about angling. There is nothing so vexing as to be worried with advice
and suggestions from superficial anglers – I mean those who observe little and

note still less when they go a-fishing, and think, for instance, that because chub, roach, or barbel, have once been caught in a certain place, they can always be captured there; and that, where pike may be caught in December or January, they will be found in the same locations in the autumn months, which is seldom, if ever, the case.

And so it came to pass that the keeper got severely dropped on, for he stuck close to Francis, who was carefully spinning a likely piece of water, and he kept repeating, 'You take my advice, sir, and go to the top of the lake and try there; a friend of mine, sir, last March, caught a twenty-pounder, sir, on them shallows.' At length, Francis, who could no longer endure this reiterated advice, turned round to the keeper and said, 'Confound your friend and his twenty-pound pike, and you too. If you don't hold your jaw, I'll chuck you into the water.' So the keeper departed, and left us to ourselves.

Alfred Jardine, *Pike and Perch*, 1898.

A Thames Gudgeon Party

In my earliest memories of the Thames the gudgeon is associated with fishing parties, love-making, and a dinner at the local hotel, in which this dainty fish was, as the whitebait is at Greenwich, the most talked of dish. The first week in September was the favourite time for gudgeon contests, punt against punt, in each of which were fishermen, lady angler, and gentleman ditto. The winners laughed and joked and, in some instances, boasted a little; the losers paid the bill.

A Party Angling. An engraving after a painting by G. Morland

Fish Tales

Try to realise a day on the Thames – there were no rowdies or hooligans then – with her whose company you would most desire on such an occasion, while other punt or punts are similarly manned and on a like quest. All have started with smiling faces, and ladies a little flushed with the excitement of the coming contest.

How the fishermen would rake and rake and how quickly bait the lady's hook; and rake again, until the fish had gathered from so far as the cloudy water had travelled to tell them that there was a disturbance above that must mean food!

No sport is so sure, no fish a bolder biter; the little cork float, weighted almost to vanishing point, will disappear, time after time, until it may be you have many dozens from your first pitch.

At times a shoal of perch attracted by the movement of gudgeon and minnows, will head up, and then you will be pleased with the delight of your lady should she be the first to get one. While the perch are there slyly keep your hook unbaited, it won't be for long, and watch her face for your reward.

A landing for lunch and another for tea are almost begrudged, and, last of all, comes a comparison of catches; no, not last, for there is the dinner yet to eat with three of its items unvarying, gudgeon, partridge, and champagne.

How the old-fashioned puntsmen enjoyed those times may be gathered from their regrets that such parties are now very rare and that the gudgeon is passing through a long period of neglect.

Not long since, four of us decided on another friendly match of this sort to see if the sport was really what our memories painted it.

It was a real old type of professional I patronised; one who, I knew, would be pleased to talk of gudgeon and of old times to me. Indeed, I remembered his tongue, once started, used to be very hard to stop, so I thought it best to warn my companion of this failing that she might use her woman's wit to stop him if need arose. He and I had fished much together, braved bad weather and numerous failures. So I was pleased to see him again and glad, of course, to hear him say:

'Why, bless me! sir, you look younger than ever.' The telling of this fib, at which I was silly enough to look pleased, started him:

'Good morning, ma'am; allow me. Handing the ladies in and out is one of our old customs and privileges for which I am a stickler. I am not so slippery shod or fingered as your London gents.'

'Do you think the gudgeon are likely to bite today?' was the answer to his opening, a kindly-meant effort, no doubt to stem or, at any rate, to steer the old man's tongue. 'You may not know it, ma'am, but so long as you do me the honour to come in my punt, I am the responsible party.' Then turning to me, 'Your chief duty, sir, will be to see you do not miss a bite; I'll look after the lady. Why, only the other day I had a young married couple out with me jack fishing; the husband got a run, hooked a fish, and before I could get the net out, lifted a four-pounder bang in betwixt and between the lady's legs. The lady . . .'

'Oh, what is that bird over there?'

'A moorhen, ma'am.'

'Let's go quietly and see how close we can get to it.'

Our man was not easy to stop, but he was well-bitted that day; indeed he did little talking, for him, and he worked the rake so well that our rivals had to pay the bill, which, of course, included the usual dinner.

Philip Green, *What I have Seen While Fishing*, 1924.

A Christmas Morning's Chubbing

Winter chub fishing may not appeal to the angler who considers sport to be nothing more or less than lying full length on the banks of some river trying to shade himself from the rays of a scorching sun.

If there was one sport more than another that I used to delight in, that one was to find myself on the banks of a good running river, with the water in splendid order; a good supply of bait, the weather clear, crisp, and with a suspicion of frost, and the chub inclined to my way of thinking. There is no branch of angling in all the catalogue of the varied styles that brings out the capabilities, the skill, and the dexterity in handling his tools more, than does this stream-fishing with a float for chub.

F i s h   T a l e s

It was a typical Christmas morning of the good old-fashioned sort; a slight misty haze, aided by a frost, had clothed the trees and hedges in a fantastic garb of glittering, scintillating white. Scarcely a breath of wind was blowing, but what there was brought with it in the face of the early morning sportsman a taste of the coldness of the north. The sun was just rising above the spur of a range of low hills that flanked the south-eastern horizon, and gleamed with a dull misty red, throwing a series of strange lights and shadows across its track, and lighting up in a brilliant silvery sheen the tops of the distant trees. Underfoot the grass crunched with every step, and all along the river's edge, and clinging lovingly to the lowest twigs of the overhanging scattered bushes, was a thin skim of ice, that swayed and dipped with every swirl of the current.

It most certainly was not a morning for a butterfly fisherman to be out, whose idea of fishing was green trees and leaves, to be lulled into sleep by a lazy drone from a thousand insects, under a cloudless sun. I was a bit younger and more hardy on the day that I have in my mind's eyes just now, and rather gloried in the beauties of a keen winter's morn, and considered a day's chubbing under the conditions of that day the very beau-ideal of a sportsman's life; for be it known to all and sundry that our leather-mouthed friend the chub is the sporting fish par excellence of a keen and frosty day, pike and grayling not excepted, by me at any rate.

I had left the people of the house that Christmas morn – the women folk, at any rate – a clear field and no favour to prepare the turkey, the plum-pudding, and the various indigestible items that go to make up that time-honoured meal known as the Christmas dinner. Strict orders and sundry injunctions had been given as to the time to return, and an hour later I stood in the valley of the grand old river Trent, watching the wintry sun climbing slowly up the distant hill, and lighting up the whole landscape in a glorious halo of dancing white. The river flowed along, curling under the roots of those old bushes, ever and anon swirling with a gurgling splash as an eddy was sucked underneath the hollow clay bank, then swirled on again until finally lost under the dark shadows of a distant bough. It was extremely inviting, in spite of its somewhat wintry aspect. The water was just tinged with a very faint colour: a stone on the bottom could be detected about two feet down.

Chub are a fish that can be found in a suitable place during very cold and frosty weather, even when the place is not more than three or four feet deep. It is a mistake to think that chub can only be found in very deep water during the cold weather; I have found them at all depths, when the float had to be fourteen feet away from the hook, and when it was only two feet away. This particular part of the river, under the boughs and overhanging banks, varied from two to five feet in depth, and contained some pretty fair fish, as previous visits and experiences had more than once clearly proved, and I looked forward to an enjoyable, not to say an exciting time.

If there is one bait more than another that I swear by for the fish now under notice, when weather is cold and frosty, that bait is bullock's pith, raw, for the hook, and bullock's brains, boiled hard and finely minced, for ground-bait, if that particular operation can be called ground-baiting. It was rather a difficult job, getting that bait on Christmas Eve, but by great good luck a butcher friend obliged me with a set. The brains were well washed and cleaned, all the blood and impurities being carefully removed; they were then tied up in a square of calico and boiled for nearly an hour, until they became tough and hard.

The pith itself, which I suppose I need not say is the spinal cord of the beast, was skinned, divided into short ropes as it were, and well washed and cleaned. This is all that is required; the inner fine skin is useful for holding the bait more firmly on the hook, the coarse, rough outside skin only being removed.

It was a morning made for chub fishing – water in the very best condition, and a stream running that was strong enough to carry the float and tackle onward without check or hindrance. This combination of affairs suggested an enjoyable time, and something to show for it at the end. The first place I tried was along the front of a low overhanging bank, crowned with a couple of bush-es whose lowest boughs touched the water some four feet out in the stream: water about the same number of feet deep.

Taking out the shell and scissors, I put a bit of the boiled brains about the size of a large walnut in the former and clipped it up as small as ever I could, then putting sufficient water in the shell to cover the brains, well stirred and mixed them together, finally throwing the contents of the shell a few yards higher up stream, so that it would reach midwater or a little deeper by the time it got to the bushes, taking care that it sank a foot or so in front of the boughs and whirled about the stream in tiny fragments. If you are careful where you throw the clipped-up brains and mix and stir well in a little water, they will sink attractively, exactly where you want them.

My pith was in short ropes about six or eight inches long, and say half an inch thick. Clipping a bit off about three-quarters of an inch long, I inserted the hook two or three times, until the bait was worked up the shank, and no more long ends hanging loose below the bend than could possibly be helped.

Then I stood well up above the stream, gently tossing out the tackle so that the float would travel some foot or eighteen inches in front of the boughs, with the bait about six inches above the bottom (hitting that distance nicely), taking care that the float did not travel quite so fast as it would have liked to do. This gentle holding back of the float causes the bait to travel a little in advance, and the strike, when a fish takes it, is more sharp and direct. Now this is most important in any sort of stream-fishing, when the float must of necessity be a good distance below where you stand: the bait must not trail behind the float.

Steadily onward went that float, three quarters of an inch of its red tip showing above the water, until it reached about the centre of the first bush, when it shot suddenly downwards with that sideways glide so characteristic of a chub bite when he means business. An instantaneous response from the rod-point resulted in a heavy plunge and a tackle as fast as a thief in a mill, which no amount of sawing this way and that could loosen. I have heard my old friend, the late Tom Sunman, say that a chub hardly ever takes bait the first time it goes past him; he simply looks out for a convenient stump or root, and next time, seizing the bait, dashes headlong round its chosen retreat.

Anyhow, there it was, a bad start; the first swim down had resulted in a lost fish and a broken tackle. Luckily the hook itself only had gone, so it was very easy to repair the damages.

The swim being hopelessly disturbed for the time being, I went on to a nice little eddy that curled inside a hollow shelving bank. Repeating the operation that had led to such a disastrous result before, the bag speedily had its first occupant. Ten more minutes' careful trail there failed to add a companion to its lonely condition. The three next swims and more than half an hour's work also failed to produce any results whatever, and I began to think that after all the bag would be extremely light.

A little lower down stream, at the corner of a small spinney, was a short length of old decaying camp-shedding, with one or two rather dangerous fasteners projecting from it. This swim was a little deeper than the usual run just there, and it looked so tempting that I determined to give it a little extra ground-bait and a more extended trial, in spite of the fine skins of ice that encrusted every rotten timber and threatened to cut asunder the line if the fish bolted for that particular bit of cover. I got here the best brace of the day, both well over the three pounds, and had two rather bad smashes among these villainous piles, stones, sunken timber, and old iron bolts.

About fifty yards lower down stream the bank suddenly rose to a height of nine or ten feet; a heavy flood some time or other had there swept out a little sheltered bay, into which the stream raced with considerable force, forming a beautiful umbrella-like eddy that curled and dimpled round and round, edging a mass of yeast-like foam six inches up the steep bank on the opposite corner. This swim was about three feet deep, and always worth trying. But now a two-pounder only rewarded my very best efforts.

A distant village clock, through the clear winter atmosphere, now chimed out the hour, and reminded me that our Christmas fishing trip was rapidly drawing to a close, and that it would soon be time to pack up and away. There was just time to try the bushes where four hours earlier I had had my first

mishap; so I retraced my steps, passing the succession of curling eddies, dipping boughs, old wooden camp-shedding, and rattling streams that had afforded me such delight during the short hours of that winter's day. This time I managed, by exercising a quick and sudden pressure, to land the brother chub to the one hooked and lost in the morning.

The rooks were homing slowly overhead, a cloud of pigeons were whirling up the slope of a distant wooded hill, and a flock of green plovers were alternately showing their black and white as they turned from side to side during their flight across the meadow on the opposite bank, when I turned away for the hour's homeward march that lay between me and that Christmas dinner, for which the day and its results had given me such an appetite. The bag contained six chub weighing close on fifteen pounds – the largest nearly three and a half pounds, smallest just under two pounds.

J.W. Martin, *My Fishing Days and Fishing Ways*, 1906.

His First Salmon

I can't begin describing today. The rainbow last night was a good sign, and I woke up feeling that it was going to be a massacre. But the window was wet and the slate sky icy. Still, it might clear at noon. We started on the Mill Pool straight away, on the assumption that one never knew. There might be. And so we cast slowly down, and the east wind blew the rain through everything, and the river was higher still (it has not yet been in good condition) and the more we cast the more it grew upon us that hope was dead. From eight-thirty until one-fifteen we wandered on the banks, like lost souls staying for waftage. It didn't clear up by noon. We tried the Crooked Pot; we tried the Ardgalleys; we tried up above the snipe marsh to the bitter end. I cracked off one of my two Kessler's Fancies. The east and watery wind blew Macdonald's casts on to the bank, to my secret joy. My mackintosh was torn at the back. I only had a cap, and that was a cold poultice. I wore it back to front, in the vain effort to keep the rain from running down my neck. I paid out a sticking line with slippery, frozen fingers: the horrible and slightly rasping stickiness of cold wet deer's fat. I snapped off one of Macdonald's flies, using the salmon rod, by catching it in the bank. I found it again, and tied it on in an ague.

At one-fifteen we had lunch. We didn't talk much. Macdonald says that witchcraft was practised about here, but it has died out. There were three curlew and a thing like a black water rat: probably a form of were-wolf.

From one-forty-five to two-thirty we dragged miserably back towards the Mill Pool. By now Macdonald was fishing in front with the fly and I was coming after him, handlining a minnow off Cheese's rod. It became really impossible to go on. I couldn't feel the line. I forget whether it was hail then or sleet. I asked Macdonald if he would mind using his spinning rod. It was a case of wanting something to do, but being unable to go on handlining. I had four casts, and caught the bottom. By now I was accustomed to this, and didn't strike. At the sixth cast I caught it again, but it was a little different. It just seemed to move: an inch, a millimetre. I struck. It couldn't be what it seemed. The line cut the water, not quite in the usual way. I could have felt, I thought I did feel that it was moving towards me. But I was not going to tell Macdonald, not yet. It was a salmon. Oh, God, it was a salmon, and it would obviously get off at once. I pulled and waited and it was coming and it didn't seem to get off. It was deep. It stayed deep.

I shouted to Macdonald, who came, thinking I was snagged. I said, 'I think I have a fish.'

He looked at me to see if I was mad, then at the line to see if he was. He said, 'You have. Yes, certainly you have.' Then he began to become hysterical. If it had been his own fish he wouldn't have minded. But he had been wanting one for me for three days, and he was terrified I would lose it. He was in agony because he said I was holding it too hard. He beseeched me to let it go. I assured him that it was quite all right. I talked conversationally about different ways of killing salmon. I asked him to look at the time. Then the fish came up for a second. Macdonald said, 'It's a big trout', and my heart went down.

I said, 'Thank God it isn't an eel.'

He said, 'But no trout would hold you down like that. It would come up and flutter on the surface.'

It was only the reddish water, the aftermath of the spate, which had made him look rusty. I played him. I was hard on him, except when he had to go. He only took me twenty yards down the bank. Macdonald kept pleading for kinder treatment, but I wouldn't. I didn't know how long it was going to go on, or what was likely to happen, but I was going to hold him tight. I became aware of that moment when the cast would snap supernaturally, and let him off at that moment.

I brought him up, and we could get a good look. He was lovely and terrible, like a shark. I knew we couldn't possibly have him. He sloughed in the water. Then he was weaker and came towards us. Then he was off. And then back slowly, but still too strong. Twice more, and he was swimming just below Macdonald. Macdonald slashed at him, and missed. I said, agonised, 'No hurry', and took him off for another circular tour. At last he was floating on his side, exactly below the executioner. This time there was no mistake. The gaff pulled like lightning: he was on the bank!

My first salmon. Ten and a half pounds. Thirteen minutes.

Incredible, but killed. I stuffed a pound into Macdonald's pocket, against his will, nearly cried, and went on fishing. Occasionally I peeped at the salmon. For some reason I didn't like to give it a close look. It would have been a kind of hubris to look at it closely. It might have vanished.

Thinking back over this incredibly wonderful experience, the only time I shall ever kill my first salmon again, several things become vivid. There was the way he took me. I understand now what fishing writers mean by a 'determined pull'. There was no grab, like a trout's. He simply took hold of me, not caught hold, and held me down. It was as if I were a small boy that he was going to spank. It was a determined outrage on my minnow, nothing wild or flashy about it at all. Then there was the extraordinary and unforced calm which descended when I knew he was on.

I felt happy and interested, as if I had been condemned to death. This changed once, when my line jammed on the handle of the reel. Then I said, 'Oh, it's jammed.' It was a lamenting squeal, and I heard my own voice. I also remember Macdonald saying, 'Well, if we can only get this one on the bank, we can call it a guid day.' The important thing was the weather. Just for that twenty minutes the wind veered west and the sun shone. It woke the salmon up and they began to move up once more. But before moving they felt lively and took. I am sure that I hooked this fish during the only three or four minutes when it would have been possible to take fish by any means. The sun went in again, the wind went east, the rain came down: but there was a silver cock salmon on the bank. The first from Craigenkillie this year.

T.H. White, *England Have My Bones*, 1936.

The Shoemaker's Monster

In the month of July, some thirty years ago, one Duncan Grant, a shoemaker by profession, who was more addicted to fishing than to his craft, went up the way from the village of Aberlour, in the north, to take a cast in some of the pools above Elchies Water. He had no great choice of tackle, as may be conceived; nothing, in fact, but what was useful, and scant supply of that. Duncan tried one or two pools without success, till he arrived at a very deep and rapid stream, facetiously termed 'the Mountebank': here he paused, as if meditating whether he should throw his line or not. 'She is very big,' said he to himself, 'but I'll try her; if I grip him he'll be worth the hauding.'

He then fished it, a step and a throw, about halfway down, when a heavy splash proclaimed that he had raised him, though he missed the fly. Going back a few paces, he came over him again, and hooked him. The first tug verified to Duncan his prognostication, that if he was there 'he would be worth the hauding'; but his tackle had thirty plies of hair next the fly, and he held fast, nothing daunted. Give and take went on with dubious advantage, the fish occasionally sulking.

The thing at length became serious; and, after a succession of the same tactics, Duncan found himself at the Boat of Aberlour, seven hours after he had hooked his fish, the said fish fast under a stone, and himself completely tired. He had some thoughts of breaking his tackle and giving the thing up; but he finally hit upon an expedient to rest himself, and at the same time to guard against the surprise and consequence of a sudden movement of the fish.

A ticklish cast. An engraving by the great Victorian illustrator, Charles Whymper

He laid himself down comfortably on the bank, the butt end of his rod in front; and most ingeniously drew out part of his line, which he held in his teeth. 'If he tugs when I'm sleeping,' said he, 'I think I'll find him noo'; and no doubt it is probable he would. Accordingly, after a comfortable nap of three or four hours, Duncan was awoke by a most unceremonious tug at his jaws. In a moment he was on his feet, his rod well up, and the fish swattering down the stream. He followed as best he could, and was beginning to think of the rock at Craigellachie, when he found to his great relief that he could 'get a pull on him'. He had now comparatively easy work; and exactly twelve hours after hooking him, he cleiked him at the head of Lord Fife's water: he weighed fifty-four pounds, Dutch, and had the tide lice upon him.

William Scrope, *Days and Nights of Salmon Fishing in the Tweed*, 1843.

Giants of the Wye

As regards the huge fish of over fifty pounds, the first of which I have any record is the legendary monster which the Hon. Geoffrey Hill, and Christmas the keeper, played all through a summer night in the Agin Pool at the Nyth; but this fish was never even seen by the angler, and therefore cannot be included in the list of real big fish. Nor can that other great 'fish' which a medico of Ross played all night long only to find in the morning that he had been anchored to a piece of fencing wire, the uneasy writhings of which had deceived him into believing they were the struggles of a salmon. Five fish only of over fifty pounds have been killed in the Wye on the rod, and the full list is as follows: The first of these huge salmon weighed fifty-one pounds and was killed by Mr J. Wyndham Smith in 191–. He killed this salmon in the famous Quarry Pool at Aramstone; and on the same morning he killed another fish of forty-four pounds. Two fish weighing ninety-five pounds and this, I believe, a record for a single day's fishing in the Wye, as regards size.

In March 1920, Colonel Tilney killed the second in Higgins Wood at Whitney, which weighed fifty-two pounds, and thereby set up a record for size

which lasted for three years, until on 13 March 1923, Miss Doreen Davey broke
the record again in the Cowpond, with a fish of fifty-three pounds, and this
record is still unbroken. I believe this is a spring record for Great Britain. This
was a magnificently proportioned salmon measuring fifty-two and a half inches
in length and twenty-nine inches in girth. It looked like a massive side of
bacon when lying on the slab and it gave her the fight of a lifetime before it
came to the gaff. Here is her own most lively account of that fight:

The 'Cowpond' begins, I believe, near my father's fishing hut, and continues
downwards for about two hundred yards of deep water with a strong current
through it – good fly water with a rough stony bottom – until it bends into
what is known locally as the 'Middle Hole'. The 'Middle Hole' always holds
fish, but only once in eighteen years has a salmon been taken there. It is a
deep, broad, swirly place, and the fish run up from it into the 'Cowpond',
probably to discuss the weather, take the air, and sometimes, I believe, to
lure the angler!

This one did so! I fished over him in the morning, for my father generally
turns me on to the best places. The salmon was probably thinking of other
things just then – perhaps of his coming honeymoon or of the vile wind
which was blowing, for he would not come and join in the sport!

I fished all day, as did my father, but nothing would respond. At about
five-thirty p.m., having lost all hope, and fully expecting to have to go home
and record another blank day, I was making a few casts while waiting for my
father to join me, and I hooked a fish on a small minnow I had put on for a
change. I adopted the usual tactics, but the fish swam about and did more or
less what he liked! I believe it is even possible that he growled at me, but a
cold northeast wind drowned the noise and so I did not hear it! He had several nice bits of exercise, but he never jumped or let me get a glimpse at
him, and I had to do practically what he suggested, for I was unable to make
any real impression on him. After about twenty minutes of this my father
came along, and I called to him to take a turn. He put on as much strain as
possible, and gave me the rod back again in about ten minutes, saying it was
my 'funeral' and so I ought to do the bulk of the work! So I went on again
for about ten minutes and then we changed once more and my father did his

best to make the fish really annoyed. We did not want him to go down the river any further, and he did not want to go up! We had been taken as far down as the river was safe.

Then we found that we could annoy the salmon best by walking him up the river with very hard pulling, and then running down with him. So we continued doing this as far as we were allowed to do it by the brute. Of course I was constantly varying the angle of the strain, so as to throw him off his balance, but he countered this by varying his position to meet what I was doing. And so it went on, and it grew darker as the twilight faded. I had to fight the daylight as well as the fish! Luckily the fish and the river were west of us and so we could see the line for quite a long time in the twilight.

Then at last, about seven o'clock, he got quite cross, running down and across the river, wallowing along the surface so that we could see him for the first time. Up to now we had only been guessing, but in the fading twilight we could see that it was really a monster reflected on the surface of the water. After this it soon got quite dark, and Jellis, father's chauffeur, had a 'brainwave'! He has been with us for about twenty years, we called him John, and he has gaffed lots of salmon. He started a large fire on the river bank, and got some paraffin and paper from the hut ready for the crucial moment when the gaff should be required.

It was a 'desperate fine battle', but the fish now had to do what we wanted him to do more often than when the fight started. We knew that if the hold was good and the tackle did not give out from the long continued strain, 'beauty would defeat the beast'! An onlooker, who had never seen a fish caught before, gave us quite an amusing turn. He thought it was about time to pour some of our precious paraffin on the fire, thinking we wanted more light. There was no one to stop him, and he did it. I can smell that funny odour of singed cloth even now!

Then my father swore! He was taking a spell at the rod, and I went to feed the fire. The tin of paraffin had been left near by with the cork out, and I accidentally kicked it over! I saved enough for the final effort, however, and father quietened down! We were joined by a fishing neighbour, Mr Barrett, and Mr Merton's gillie, Charlie Donald, who had come to see what the trouble was about, having noticed the fire and the figures moving about. They brought about four inches of candle with them – bless 'em!

The fish, by now, was making shorter journeys, and was 'jagging' badly – a most disquieting action to the angler, for it feels as though every jag must break something! The only safe thing to do, I think, is to keep the top of one's rod well up, and rather easy, allowing the top joint to do what it was intended to do.

The end came with almost dramatic suddenness. The fish took a few long lunges, rolled a bit, ran, and was pulled to the right towards the bank. Jellis crept quickly to the right, but the fish saw him cross the fire-light for he jinked, ran back and round to my left. He was steered in, and in a mix-up of splash and spray the faithful John Jellis with the gaff and Charley Donald with his hands as much round the tail of the fish as he could get them, managed to haul him out of the water. The fish was landed at seven-thirty-five and was hooked at five-forty! One hour and fifty-five minutes of concentrated excitement and real hard work! We never gave him a moment's peace, and played him hard the whole time with the sort of strain that will kill a twenty-pound fish in seven or eight minutes.

Luckily for us Mr Powell, of Winforton, who kindly allows us to leave the car with him, formed himself into a 'search party' and came to look for our corpses with a hurricane lamp, a thing anyone in our family is warned not to bother about under three days! However, we were very glad to see him and his lamp, for we were able to find our way back to the car. The fish was taken to the office of the Wye Board of Conservators the next day and was weighed and measured – weight fifty-nine and a half pounds, length fifty-two and a half inches, girth twenty-nine inches. The fish was then displayed in Hereford, an outline for a carving made, and the flesh was then sold, the proceeds to be given to the Herefordshire General Hospital.

Miss Davey's fish, monstrous as it was, pales into insignificance beside the huge and decaying corpse of a salmon which was found in the river at Evenpitt Bridge on 26 May 1920. The previous history of this fish is very mysterious and the story has almost become a legend of the past. It is believed that this enormous salmon was hooked in Lower Pike's at Whitney by General Davidson and played for a very long time until both fish and angler were exhausted. At last the trace broke and the salmon rolled away downstream. Nothing more was heard until some time later, when an enormous salmon was found lying dead in the river near Hereford. The finder measured the salmon and found that it was no less than fifty-nine and a half inches long and thirty-three and a quarter inches in girth. Measurements such as these would mean that the fish weighed in life about eighty pounds, but the mystery deepened further still. The finder went away, leaving the fish on the bank and meaning to return for it later. On his return the fish had disappeared. Evidently someone had thrown it into the river, and in the river it remained until it was discovered in a liquefying rotten condition miles further down. Even when in this terrible state and falling to pieces the fish measured fifty-seven inches long and twenty-six inches in girth.

H.A. Gilbert, *The Tale of a Wye Fisherman*, 1929.

Still life of salmon and trout on a riverbank, by J.A. Russell

Fish Tales

Fisherman's Luck!

I was forcing a greased line into the wind; and as I was wading deep the late drive required to extend the line against the gale caused the rod point to strike the water at each cast. Imagine my surprise when a salmon's head emerged just as the rod point hit the water, and seizing the tip gave it a good pull.

On another occasion I was acting as gillie for a friend, who was playing a salmon from the bank where the water was deep at the edge. There was a ripple and the light was bad, but his fish was close into shore. Seeing a salmon turn and glint, I took a chance and sinking the gaff drew it out, and there was the fish – or so I thought. But my friend was still playing his fish! I had gaffed another which had been keeping his fish company.

One day I hooked a fish on a threadline minnow. Meanwhile my greased-line fly was hanging a rod's length from the stem of my boat for the cast to soak. No sooner was the first fish hooked when another took the fly. Seizing the second rod, there I stood a rod in each hand, a salmon on each and both reels screaming – two to one! The boatman took one rod and killed the salmon, but mine came unstuck – one to two!

G.P.R. Balfour-Kinnear, *Catching Salmon and Sea-Trout*, 1938.

A Glorious Bass

Fitful gusts were coming off the land, but for the first part of our journey they troubled us little, as, with sails all set, we glided quickly out of the bay, the wind being dead aft. The bass had been playing havoc with my tackle and I was stowed away in the cuddy of the lugger mounting a Chapman spinner and arranging on it the tail of a mackerel – a capital bait for bass in those waters cut 'partail' fashion. I was deeply absorbed in the intricacies of fastening off a piece of whipping with an end all too short, when the little vessel gave a lurch, there was a fearful crash overhead and the cuddy became suddenly darkened. On attempting to grope my way out I found myself shut in by a heap of sailcloth.

Fish Tales

It was no small accident – the mast had gone overboard. While we were rounding the rocky headland known as the Monkstone, at the end of the bay, a tremendous puff of wind had come flying down a gully, hitting the mainsail like a sledge-hammer. A splicing in the stay on the windward side slipped, and the mast, having no longer any support, snapped off short. There was a strong current setting in around the point, and all haste was made to get out an anchor.

My crew consisted of a pilot and his nephew. The one, a quiet, cautious and experienced old salt, equal to any emergency; the other, young, active, and willing, and as good a lad as ever sailed in the Bristol Channel.

'If you would come ashore with me, sir,' said the nephew, 'and look after the punt, I will borrow a saw and hatchet and we will be under way again in an hour's time.' It was good news; for I quite expected this, my last day's bass fishing for the season, would have to be abandoned, as we were five miles from the fishing ground. It was then ten o'clock. The bass fed for about two hours during the strongest run of the flood tide, and if we were not on the spot by one o'clock we should be too late. While I put Harry ashore and watched over our little punt, for the tide was rising fast, our skipper remained on board, cleared the wreckage, moved the stump of the mast, and got everything ready for his nephew, who, fortunately for us, had served an apprenticeship with a ship-builder. He returned in about half an hour's time, and the end of the upper portion of the mast was soon trimmed up and carefully shaped. But it was a difficult task to replace the heavy pole. While Harry and his uncle lifted it, I hauled on to the forestay, and by degrees our 'stick', as yachtsmen say, pointed once more heavenwards. An hour later we were heading towards the bass ground, but with one reef down, for the simple reason that our mast was not long enough to carry the whole sail. I returned to the cuddy, finished arranging my tackle, and then took a turn at the helm. After all we arrived at the fishing grounds in good time.

Half a mile from the mainland stands a rocky, treeless, rabbit-haunted island, of a hundred acres or more. During the flood tide a tremendous current sweeps through the channel, and curls and twists, and boils and eddies round the shoals and sandbanks on either side of the fairway.

The local method of fishing is to cruise backwards and forwards across the current, trailing spinning bait, or strip of mackerel, or gurnard skin, or sometimes a whole but very small mackerel, called by the fishermen of those parts a 'joey'. The boat must be fast and smartly handled, and, it need hardly be said, there must be a good stiff breeze. None of these essentials was wanting, but owing to our shortened mast we were, as I have said, obliged to keep one reef in the mainsail, which, of course, handicapped us immensely. Worse than this, we were unable to shift our lug when going about, so that on one tack we practically lost about one-third of our sail area. The result was that, whenever the wind fell a little, the current caught hold of us, we lost ground, and were about a quarter of an hour in regaining the fishing ground.

As keenly interested in the bass as ourselves were about four or five hundred gulls which were dotted about the cliffs, waiting for the curtain to be raised and the play to commence. Now and then one would launch itself into the air, take a swoop down near the surface of the water, utter a cry, and then fly back again, as if to say, 'No, they have not come yet; you can stay where you are.'

So far the tide had not run very fiercely, and we had no difficulty in holding our own, for there was a good sailing breeze. On one side of the boat we had out the mackerel-tail bait, spinning splendidly on the Chapman spinner, and on the other the head of a mackerel, with about three inches of skin brought to a point – a bait with which I had killed several fish on various occasions. Gradually the current became stronger, and little eddies and whirlpools began to form over the sandbanks. Sometimes we were in these and the boat would be twisted round, and almost taken aback before we knew where we were; but we generally managed to keep in the deeper water of the channel, and let our baits play over the edges of the sandbanks. Very soon a yacht joined us, and began cruising over the bass ground – much too large a vessel for the place. One or two other boats from a fishing town sailed up, and five minutes later the fun began.

The gulls saw the fish before we did.

Suddenly there was a universal cry from the throats of the birds, and they came dashing down to the water, fighting fiercely with a shoal of bass for the unfortunate herring fry. Chased by the bass beneath, harried by the gulls above, the poor little fish had a very bad time of it. Our aim and object was to follow the gulls. Wherever they went, there, we knew, were the herring fry, and wherever the latter were, there also were the bass. It was exciting, but could hardly be called sport. There was no play – in fact, a rod was useless. The boat could not be brought to, nor could a fish be followed. The tackle had to be strong enough to bring them in willy-nilly.

First came a tremendous pull on the mackerel-tail spinning bait, and on hauling in I was disgusted to find that two hooks were broken. Nothing short of a Mahseer triangle would do for that fishing. Harry, who had hold of the line bearing the mackerel head, was more fortunate, and very steadily and quietly hauled in a bass of about three pounds. Then the wind fell somewhat, and just as we were expecting great things, we were drawn back into the swirling mael-strom, and, much to our disgust, saw the occupants of all the other boats haul-ing in fish, while we were whirled and twisted about in the boiling waters. My crew did their best, but it was a quarter of an hour or more before we again reached the scene of action. Meanwhile, having prepared another mackerel-tail bait, and fitted up the Chapman spinner with the strongest and largest trian-gles I had in my box, I was rewarded by bringing another three- or four-pound bass into the boat. And thus our sport continued, the occupants of the yacht and companion fishing-boats hauling in bass every few minutes.

If we could have held our ground I believe we should have made a splendid bag, but fortune was against us; though, all things considered, I ought to have been thankful for having done any fishing at all that day. I very much wanted the men to come to an anchor and fish with drift-lines, but they assured me that if they did the stream was so strong their anchor would drag until it fouled in a rock or stone and they might be unable to get it up again. The conclusion I came to was that a better way of fishing the ground would be with drift-lines from a small boat moored with a heavy stone.

The play ended as suddenly as it began. The water ceased to be broken by the bass, and silently and quietly the gorged gulls flitted off to their resting places among the cliffs, where, let it be hoped, 'good digestion waited on appetite'. So our helm was put down, and we left those tumultuous waters for the little haven at the end of the bay.

The wind was light and night had fallen before we turned the point off which our mishap occurred in the morning. Dotted about Saundersfoot Bay were little fires, blazing up from stoves which the herring fishermen had placed in the centre of their small open boats to temper the chilly air of an October night. We dodged the drifting nets as best we could, but sailed over one in the darkness. As we approached the old harbour we were becalmed, and Harry, putting out a long sweep, slowly brought us up to the steps at the foot of the cliff path.

John Bickerdyke, *Days of My Life*, 1895.

Bass on a Fly Rod

It is four o'clock on a July morning. The sun is still down behind Exmouth, but, as we walk a few steps to the boat-house, the haze that broods over the Den, the cloudless blue sky overhead, the stillness in the air, all forecast a scorching day. And on a hot morning, even before breakfast, we have reckoned; otherwise, a suit of ducks over one's pyjamas would be light attire for early morning on the water. As a matter of fact, until the sun gets over the elms, there is a nip in the air that occasionally takes our thoughts to the long coat that hangs behind the door.

A little after four, having aroused Cox, who like the May Queen has to be awakened early if he is to get up at all, and given him time for his inevitable cup of stewed and syrupy tea, we are snug in the *Hirondelle*, our trout rods and traces of single gut ready for action, and a bait-box towing alongside with a score of dashing sand-eels fresh from the night's seine. It will be high water soon after nine, so that the tide must have turned an hour ago, and indeed it is draining perceptibly in from the sea, as witness the boats that have swung round to it. Yet there will not be enough for an hour at least to take our boat along stern-first, which is the ultimate position in which we have to fish for the bass on the rough ground above the yachts.

We shoot out from the landing-place, and just above us lie great merchant-men in tiers, flying the flags of half a dozen nations. At so early an hour this fleet shows no sign of life, unless indeed a mongrel cur barks at us from the bows of some vessel close to which we pass, to be chastised later, no doubt, for having disturbed the sleep of everyone on the river. Later, when we have fished for a couple of hours, there will be activity and bustle, sleepy lads scrubbing down the decks, men ashore hailing whichever ship they want to board and, if not quickly fetched off, adding to their humble petition and prayer such piercing expletives as might reach the ferryman of Styx.

As we first approach the lowermost tier, however, all is silence. We cannot drift the way we like until the tide runs swifter, so Cox will for forty minutes or so row the boat slowly and in circles abreast of these lower ships and the railway quay. We shall not hook anything large, but our baits are over the side now, and one never knows. Ha! what was that? A twitch of the rod-top . . . another . . . down it goes, for the slight turn of the wrist has hicked the sharp hook in beyond the barb, and the bass is fast. The reel sings a modulated hymn of praise, not raising its voice as it would if turned by a heavier fish; and the slender rod bobs, not indeed with the steady curve that tells of a big one, but sufficiently to suggest a pounder.

To bring such a bass to the net is child's work. In vain it eddies and circles round the stern. The little bronze reel is wound in almost without a hitch, and at just the right moment Cox has shipped his oars and dipped the landing-net under a gleaming little bass of perhaps a pound and a half. One does not fetch out the steelyard to these small fry, though such a fish is as pretty and as sporting as any of its size. Trout, someone murmurs? Speak up; and remember that, though we use a trout-rod, the cast is of salmon-gut, for to trust to anything finer would be to run needless risk with that record fish of the season, to dream of which means inexpensive bliss. Hook a bass like him that lies shining in the boat, quieted with the merciful tap of a rowlock, on a moorland trout cast. Hook him, if you like, but play him in a bath if you want him, for he would break your gossamer gut for all your arts.

Another sand-eel on the hook, and once more to turn our back on Cox, who again dips the paddles gently in the stream. Three or four more bass, a little smaller than the first, are hooked during the next half hour. And now the salt water is flooding the estuary in earnest; the boat drifts yards upstream each time Cox drops the sculls for the landing-net; and away now to the rough ground, just below the bridge, where, undisturbed by the salmon-nets, the big bass lie in wait for the shoals of brit that come, reckless of their doom, on the rising tide.

Fish Tales

As we pass the topmost ships, with only a couple of yachts between us and the bridge, the dripping bait-box is hauled inside the boat, and the largest sand-eels are picked out from the wriggling mass, for big bass like big fare, and if the giants are to be tempted, we must offer them the best we have. Instead of trailing the baits, as I did for the smaller game below, I now pay it out, little by little, an inch or two of the line being pulled off the reel at a time. This I go on doing mechanically, while Cox just dips the paddles so as to keep the boat back ever so little, that the line may run out as straight as a wire. Past the tennis-courts we go, looking through the arches of the bridge at the purple line of the tors on Dartmoor, and now the baits must be thirty yards away from us. There is a slight check, the merest irregularity, which would not be noticed by anyone new to the game, but which we know so well that instinctively the left hand tightens on the butt, while the right hovers above the reel. There it is! Down goes the top, no bobbing this time, but the deliberate curve to the water's edge. Murder! screams the winch, no half-hearted burr of the check like that evoked by the little fish, but a sustained crescendo note, while the line grows so rapidly less on the spinning axle that it looks as if the fish is going to break me.

Once, and once only, thank goodness, that did actually befall me on this spot. What manner of fish it may have been, I cannot, without having a glimpse of it, positively say. Local opinion favoured a salmon, but more probably it was a monster 'cobbler' bass. It simply took the bait by the lowest buoys, opposite the cricket ground, started away at lightning speed, and, as the song says, 'never stopped running till it got home'. It ran two yards of gut and one hundred yards of line to their full limit without a pause and then, without apparent effort, went on, fortunately breaking the line so near the hook that my loss of tackle was small. Other bass I have lost in that stream, but that is the first and last of any size that fought invisible.

The fish that I have hooked here by the buoy, though a powerful fighter, is not an adversary of such extreme mettle, for already he has halted in his mad career, a respite of which I take advantage to reel in half a dozen yards. Steady there! A fish of such size must be wound in gingerly, with caution, and the hand must be ever on and off the winch, winding only when the fish is so minded, since at this early stage of the struggle a direct clash of wills would mean disaster. Away goes the bass again, with strength renewed by its brief rest. Its yielding was but a feint, and this time it runs out twice as much line as I reeled in, and so is further from the boat than ever. Another halt, another reeling in; and now we are nearly up to the bridge, for all the time the boat has drifted along. For a moment I am undecided whether to shoot through the middle arch and kill the fish above the bridge, but that means losing time, so 'This side, Cox!' I say; and Cox understands, with the knowledge born of many such encounters, that he is to back the boat into the shallows on the railway side. It is there, under the windows of the early train, that the last stand is made. Gallantly the bass disputes every yard, for he is fighting for his last chance now, and he knows it. Gradually, and with fewer interruptions, I get the fine line back on the reel, and now his green head can be seen on the surface, shaking the worrying hook, as a terrier shakes a rat, and now and then making a futile attempt at retreat. In vain, such tactics! The line is tested, the hook tempered; and at last, with a final protest that spins the reel for twenty revolutions, the fish rolls on his side, and the ready landing-net is beneath it, the handle straining with the weight as Cox lifts what looks like a good ten-pounder over the side. A powerful fish, even out of the water; and the head has to be gripped firmly between the knees while the hook is taken out of the angle of the jaw, and the steelyard, confirmed later when we got ashore, registers eleven and a quarter pounds, a noble fish and the best I ever took on the rod in that river.

F.G. Aflalo, *The Salt of my Life*, 1905.

'I am Afraid it is a Shark!'

We travelled to Marco, a little settlement fringed round with coconut palms, one stormy afternoon in a small boat, and we spent that night at a little store, a rough shanty, but well equipped nevertheless. One could purchase all the needs of a rude civilisation at this place. The Seminole Indians obtain many of their goods there, and give in exchange skins of their own tanning, some most admirably prepared.

Our company was rough and much of the type so well described by Bret Harte and other Western authors. Still, our host did his best to make us comfortable, and his little daughter rose early to prepare us a breakfast. Afterwards we proceeded with our guide, Tom Hart, a man who can always be heard of at Marco, who knows the whole coast well and is an admirable fellow, to a spot at which, the previous year, he assisted to gaff three fish in a single day. Our lunch consisted of green coconuts, a small sackful of Florida oranges, cold venison (venison is the staple diet in this part of Florida), biscuits, together with many bottles of ginger ale which we had brought with us; for this part of Florida is under the 'Prohibition Law'.

The morning opened grandly. It was perfectly calm, the sunshine was brilliant, and I was strongly reminded of the Nile on a March day. Yet Hart was dissatisfied. As we made our way up the beautiful creek, I looked at as much of the horizon as I could see, but there was not so much as a cloud of the size of a man's hand. We proceeded in a leisurely manner, stopping now and then to dip our great palmetto hats into the water, in order that we might keep our heads a little cool, for the heat even at ten o'clock was almost too much for endurance.

We had gone about a mile, and Hart was resting on his oars for a moment, when on a sudden, within three feet of the boat, there was a huge swish and swirl – a miniature maelstrom for a moment – and there appeared a great black back and huge projecting fin.

'Tarpon,' said Hart.

It was my first sight of a big fish, and I must frankly confess that I felt nervous when I looked at my comparatively small rod and its frail line. He must have been a daring fellow who first thought of killing a tarpon with rod and reel. Presently, the excitement of the sport was upon me. We went as rapidly as possible up the creek and anchored under the lee of an island. During the night Hart had gone out with his casting net and captured a couple of dozen mullet, varying in size from twelve to eighteen inches. In an instant he had his knife out, and off came the head of a mullet.

Then he threaded the hook through it with a large skewer, attached the leather trace to the line, and cast for me – not a long cast, perhaps twenty-five or thirty yards. The bait sank to the bottom, and I sat with the check off the reel, and some loose line gathered in the boat, awaiting events.

Fish Tales

It was early yet. Now and then in the distance you could see a great swirl in the water, and a tarpon rose, but they kept clear of our boat. We sat smoking in the brilliant sunshine, and at the end of twenty minutes I reeled in and found that my bait had been swallowed by a huge shell-fish, a conch. It weighed between seven and eight pounds, and we had to cut it open before we could get the hook out of it. It was not unlike a gigantic whelk. This was an amusing but not a brilliant beginning. We put on fresh bait, moved forty or fifty yards, and cast in again. The day was getting hotter, and the big fish began to rise (for air) very numerously. After a time we took to counting the rises, and I am not exaggerating when I say that within sight of my field-glasses – we could see close upon a mile in one direction – over fifty distinct black fins showed during that morning.

Another cigar, the decapitation of another mullet, a fresh cast, and we settled down to watch the dial of my reel. I found Hart a pleasant and remarkably well informed person. There were few modern books of adventure with which he was not acquainted, though not many authors could have produced a more exciting tale than the history of this man's life, spent as it was in exploring the vast unknown recesses of the Everglades in search of the egret's plumes, with which fashionable ladies adorn their hats and hair. His existence had been hard and solitary, and, though he is now attaining a certain prosperity, he has spent some thousands of nights camping out alone in that strange snake- and panther-ridden country.

Our chat is cut short, however, by a sudden disappearance of the loose line over the side of the boat. Then the reel began to run out like lightning. The excitement of the moment was terrific. One's first salmon, one's first tarpon, one's first tiger, are, I should imagine, the most tremendous moments in a career of sport.

I struck, and within some fifty yards from the boat but in quite a contrary direction from that in which the line was running out, a monster fish leapt from the water. Immediately at the beginning of the run Hart had pulled up the anchor and we were drifting. When he saw the direction in which the fish had leapt he looked grave. The line, covered with sea-weed, had sagged tremendously: he feared that the fish had dropped the bait, and he was right. I wound up and found that my intended victim had seized the mullet and, in that curious way fish have, had ejected it some feet up the line. We were gloomy and disappointed.

Still, the day was young and the fish were rising numerously, though it is by some guides not considered a good sign when they are on the top of the water. I cast in again, and almost before the bait had got to the bottom it was taken. When the correct one hundred yards of the reel line had run out I struck. There was the usual commotion at the top of the water, though not exactly a leap, and we both thought that I was in for a tarpon. The fish, whatever it was, swam hither and thither at lightning speed, and then on a sudden it stopped. I struck again, knowing that if it were a tarpon the pain would cause it to rise to the top and leap. It did not do so.

'I am afraid it is a shark, sir,' remarked my guide.

I can assure those who have never killed a shark on a line that this particular fish gave me any amount of excitement. Hart rowed as fast as he could, and I reeled in rapidly to gain line, for woe betide the tarpon or shark fisher if his line is overrun. I got within probably thirty yards of the fish, when he was off again, and he ran down a branch creek for close upon half a mile. A big shark can tow a boat a very considerable distance; but there seems to be one way of tiring him, and that is, to get to one side of him, and then, using one's rod as a lever, swing round and pull against him with all one's force. In course of time that seems to exhaust him, and, revolver ready, one can reel him in, shoot him through the nose, and let him go down with the current, to be torn to pieces by his voracious brothers. My shark was evidently tired when we got up to him, and I could see his great seven-foot body looming green and hideous beneath the water. What a loathsome-looking monster a shark is! It is said that he has the cruellest teeth and eyes and the smallest heart of anything that swims. As I drew him up I thought he was practically dead. I made a shot, but, owing to the rocking boat and the excitement of the moment, was not sufficiently accurate. I hit him in the back of the neck. For a moment I thought the boat was upset. He lashed the blood-stained water furiously, and the reel, upon which I had put the check, gave such a screech as I have never heard from any reel before. He ran out some hundred and fifty yards of line, but as I drew up to him again he was obviously getting tired. There is a mental process in angling which enables one to know when one has at last gained mastery of one's fish, and so it was with this shark.

I got him up to the top of the water again. He made a violent struggle when he saw the boat, but this time my aim was truer, and I put three shots through his nose. To Hart was accorded the unpleasant task of extracting the hook from this monster.

We had wandered completely out of our course. No tarpon were known to be in the water near us, and we were thinking of returning; but despite the bright sunshine a change had come over the weather, and I know of no part of the world in which the weather alters more rapidly than in southern Florida. The wind was sighing in the mangrove trees, and though the sun shone as brightly as ever, the air grew strangely chilly. By the time we had gone back the mile we had lost, Hart was despondent. There were no tarpon rising. All we could see was a great porpoise, which rose within a few yards of us, blowing as emphatically as a steam engine.

'I am afraid we shall get no more sport to-day,' remarked Hart.

And he was right. We fished for another hour until the storm had come upon us, and then we turned back to Marco.

A.C. Harmsworth, quoted in John Bickerdyke's *Sea Fishing*, 1895.

Tarpon Fishing in Lagos

The following, written in the form of a series of letters, has all the flavour of those far-off days of sport in the Empire. The extract is from The Letters of Two Fishermen.

Lokoja, West Africa 1914

Dear Charles,

You will see from my address that I am travelling again. As a matter of fact I am on my way back from Lagos where I have been for a couple of months on special work. I had quite a good time, plenty to do in the day-time and free week-ends to do what I liked in.

Fish Tales

Lagos is the same as ever, hasn't changed one little bit from the first time I went there, four years ago. Naturally, I hadn't been there long before I began poking about to see if anybody had been sea fishing, but still found the same blissful ignorance as prevailed on my last visit. Harbour works certainly very much extended, but I hear they are getting trouble with silting and will have to build out an easterly arm – some job, looks for life.

I found the same old native fisherman who catered for me on my first visit, and my general purpose man got busy and found me a dug-out which would take me out fishing. This was an opportunity not to be despised, so I clinched the arrangements entered into by Hassan, my man. One trouble was that I know very little of their language, and they couldn't understand a word of Hausa, the language I know fairly well. However, Hassan seems to be able to make known my wants.

I used my heaviest greenheart spinning rod and largest spinning reel with heavy wire traces, and my home-made spinners, the gear I had been using for the big Giwan Rua, so felt really ready for the big stuff.

The first time we went out from the breakwater we began trolling, with the sea beautifully calm and as blue as turquoise under the early morning sun. Both men paddled well with long, easy strokes, quite different from our up-river boys, so that my bait did its work properly. I was so eager to begin that I hadn't really had time to get my few things put shipshape when I got such a wrench on the rod. I grabbed it of course and nearly turned the canoe over.

These canoes are very gimcrack affairs with only a foot freeboard, no keel, just hewn out of a tree with rough shapings for a bow and a stern. I sit flat in the bottom, facing astern, as I cannot kneel for long periods like my men do.

My fish went completely away, going so fast that my rod top was drawn down into the sea, and I could not for the life of me hold him, although I had the palm of my hand on the rim of the revolving drum of the reel until it nearly burnt into the flesh. I was only too glad when the fish stopped, and I could get my rod up to a safe angle. Almost before I could get my wits together the fish came towards me and passed right under the canoe. I seemed to reel for hours before the rod bent violently and away he went again.

F i s h   T a l e s

This went on for ages, until I began to feel really annoyed that I couldn't subdue him. I put every bit of my strength into it until I thought the rod couldn't have stood the strain any longer, but would have gone at one of the joints. This, I think, really took all the strength out of him, and we got him so near that I could see his dim shape weaving about below us. He turned to and fro, but had to come up and was got on board by Hassan.

I was fully convinced that I had hooked the father of all whales, but the fish didn't weigh more than thirty-two pounds when we killed him. He was a deep fish, slate blue on top, with a blunt head and finlets like a mackerel, also the forked tail of that family. Here I had been nearly an hour over this small fish, and was thoroughly done, so what was I going to be like if I got into a real big one, which was my idea in life at that time? However, this was much better than our previous experiences. When I was having a rest I saw a lot of silvery-looking fish jumping out of the water. They jumped out in a flock, so we went over to have a look. These fish, I should judge, were from six to twelve inches in length, swimming together in shoals. I was watching them with interest, really thinking what excellent bait they would be, when we saw a great rush into the middle of them, and out came the flock, wildly leaping from their pursuers. This meant business, so I rigged up another bait, and the two men took the dug-out round the outskirts of the shoal.

I could see down in the clear water dark blue shapes flashing underneath, so let the bait down astern. I distinctly saw three go for my bait; one got it, and away he went, but I only saw the belly flash of the other two out of the corner of my eye, as I had on my hands quite enough trouble for the immediate future. I never dreamt a fish had so much strength. When I tried to hold him he pulled yards off with savage primitive tugs. The upper threequarters of my rod was horizontal to the water with the strain, and I held on, feeling quite a void round my heart region. When nearly two hundred yards had gone he stopped, but before I could congratulate myself he was away again, but this time my canoe boys had got the hang of things and gave me help by following the fish.

At the end of the second run my fish came clear out of the water and tugged until the line twanged and vibrated with the strain. I couldn't help letting out a yell. The fish never eased up, and I finally fought him back by instinct and not with a reasoning mind. I was really feeling physically distressed when I realised he was near the canoe and Hassan got him out.

This was a different fish from the other. He was long and slim like a torpedo, blue black on top with a silver belly flushed with yellow right down to the tail, which was forked like a mackerel, and I am sure this fish is the American Yellowtail. He was forty-five pounds when weighed, and I truly had had enough, especially as we were too far from land for my liking.

The men paddled for the shore whilst I got my strength back. With these two magnificent fish on board I really couldn't bear to put a bait over and have another shot. I was sitting watching the water when, bang, I had another run, and the business began all over again, but this fish fought deep down nearly under the canoe. Things went on as I have described before, and I was fairly on top of my fish when he suddenly woke up and ran yards off. I gave him hell but could not make any impression, although he was coming up to the surface with a rush.

I was watching the rod tip when Hassan, with a chorus from the other men, yelled and pointed to a big fin sticking out of the water about one hundred yards away. I realised that the owner of that fin and myself were connected in some way and also that it was a shark. It took about three seconds for my mind to go over all the shark incidents I had ever read about, and I was not comforted. Still, something had to be done, as the shark wasn't doing anything much, and the only place my men wanted to go to was 'Home, sweet Home' in the shortest time possible.

I therefore held hard, and nothing occurred. I might be holding hard until now for all the good I was doing. However, things did move; the line went slack, and the fin moved out seawards. I reeled in with a huge sigh and soon saw I was reeling in the head and shoulders only of my fish; the other part was also going seawards.

However, our troubles were only beginning, as when the fish's head got near a great shape came from under the canoe. My fish's head and shoulders disappeared into the shape, and my reel began to spin round faster than anybody could have thought possible. I had really and truly hooked a shark, but what the devil to do with him I hadn't the foggiest notion. There may be a book written on shark fishing to help soft-headed amateurs like myself when in such trouble, but if there is I have never read it. I simply clung on for all my life. Then the brute began to run. I felt a tremendous jar on my left arm and shoulders, the dug-out gave a lurch, and my rod came back straight. I never said 'Thank God' with such thankfulness before, and believed every letter of those two small words.

I was feeling pretty frightened myself, but on turning round with a sickly grin I found three absolutely terrified guides; so I took courage as I realised there were three more frightened men in my little world than I myself. There was no more fishing, and no urging was wanted on my part until we arrived at the shore.

My legs felt quite shaky on landing, so we found a shady spot and had lunch. Through Hassan I had a long talk with the men and finally, after treating them well in the matter of a monetary present, got them to promise they would be there the next Sunday. They took the yellowtail, whilst I took the other fish, which was quite good eating. I felt the effects next day on my shoulders, and also in my groin, where the butt of the rod rested during my fishing. I therefore tied a piece of stuffed leather as big as a tennis ball on to the butt end of the rod to act as a cushion, and it was a great success, but even then there is a danger that one might hurt one's inside.

When out the next Sunday morning we didn't get any luck until we saw a school of small fish being crashed, and, as soon as we could troll a bait round the school, I got a run, which resulted in a twenty-five pound yellowtail. By the time the fight was over the school had either gone a long distance out to sea or gone down for good. Owing to my crazy craft I was frightened to go out far to sea in case of accidents, as if we got upset there were too many sharks, so we kept as near to the bar as possible. This day I saw some fish leaping clear out of the water in magnificent jumps, so we trolled round the neighbourhood and got into one without much difficulty. There was a terrific long run, and then out of the water and up into the air came five feet of silver. The fish seemed to my astonished eyes to go up and up, but when he came down again the line was slack. On examining the bait, I found the hook of the tail triangle, although it was of large dimension, pulled out straight. I then removed all three triangles and used one large hook, a number ten nought, and again tried my luck. I got another strike, so gave it back to him; another long run, then out of the water again came the fish with his mouth wide open, rattling his gills.

At the top of the jump I saw my hook flung quite another twenty feet into the air. I yelled like an Indian, when the beggar jumped, quite involuntarily.

As there seemed quite a number of these fish about working on the bar, I baited up again and got another strike, with a repetition of the jumping performance, but this time the line whistled when he entered the water again. By encouraging my men we settled down to the fight. Seven times the fish came out of the water, sideways, all ways; but I felt he was weakening himself by these acrobatics and felt confident he was ours.

The fish went finally deep and was really coming in when I felt an irresistible force take and shake it like a terrier does a rat. The line went slack, and we got in a bleeding head and a small part of the shoulders only. I could have wept with annoyance, but could only swear hard to relieve my feelings. It seems as if every fish as soon as it is weak or fights down will be taken by those accursed brutes. We never got another run. I am convinced these fish which jump so are tarpon, as they are just like those described in Dimmock's book of the tarpon; but I did not know they were on this coast.

The dredger Egerton was working on the bar, so I went alongside, and the officers gave me a whisky and soda. It's not my habit to drink before sundown, but I wanted it quite badly. The Egerton officers had been watching my efforts and were greatly interested, but confirmed the shark question. I went home afterwards, real tired.

Next Sunday there were big long swells coming over the bar, so I dared not risk going out in the dug-out. I therefore went and fished off the beach into the surf with very little hope of getting anything. I got however two good runs and two good fish of a nice size, about twenty pounds each, in the first hour. These fish were of a fine shape, silvery with darker backs, the most noticeable feature being a dull copper colour diffused all over the back of the fish. I wish I had some book which told me what they were.

As things were quite bright I was well on the *qui vive* when I felt my bait picked up, then dropped, then picked up again, and the fish moved off with due deliberation. I let him go for ten or fifteen yards, then struck hard. Nothing occurred, and I waited quite a time for action, then struck again. Things then moved, and my fish went sailing majestically parallel to the coast, about seventy yards out, like a tug, and I was forced to trot along the beach after him. The whole thing was rather ridiculous if there had been an onlooker to see it, but there was only Hassan.

Nearly a mile I trotted down the beach, then we returned the same way for some more exercise, until I began to feel a lack of breath; so I stood my ground, only to get a most violent rush which changed the trotting to a fast run. Even then I wasn't holding line. These proceedings went on, I should think, for an hour until I began to see red spots in my eyes. I gave him everything in a desperate effort. I found he was now coming in to me, so I continued until my back nearly broke. On the second breaker we saw a triangular fin and knew our old enemy the shark was around. The next time we surged on the furrow of the wave I realised we had hooked a shark all the time. I felt a real rage which gave me strength, and I laid into that fish with demoniacal strength until he came in on the last breaker of the surf. What to do with him I didn't know, as I couldn't hold him against the ebb of the surf, and he was done as we saw him roll over several times. The two fishermen with Hassan however followed the wave down, got hold of his tail, and, much to my astonishment, with the incoming surf beached him. I was scared stiff, but they did it off their own bat.

My legs shook so much now it was all over that I hastily sat down whilst my shoulders ached until I could have shouted. The fit passed off, so I went to see my catch. It was a shark all right, quite ten feet long, grey on the back with a white belly. I judged it a sand shark, but what species I don't know. He must have weighed over three hundred pounds and was far and away the biggest fish I had ever caught, bigger in fact than my wildest dreams. My rod had a curve in it like a hoop, but it came right again during the week with a weight tied on it and hung up.

That ended the day for me. The fishermen took the shark off, after getting aid, and, I believe, sold it piecemeal. Anyway, I got my own back on one of the shark family, but I have no great wish to do it all over again, especially as the tackle which I had is not to my mind suitable for the job.

I went out twice more in the dug-out. The first time I lost three of the tarpon with sharks; one brute evidently got the hook into his mouth and steamed out towards the open sea. I luckily had a knife and cut adrift before matters became more serious. I lost over a hundred yards of my twenty-four thread line which makes things too expensive, especially out here, so I am reduced to trade line which is really light cord, but if dressed is not too bad. I cannot get so much on my reel which rather cramps my style. The second time we started out with a tarpon which changed into a shark. This brute did nothing whatsoever, so we paddled up with great caution. I have ceased to rush things out here. I saw his long grey bulk with the line running to his head, then underneath him, but with no signs of the tarpon. He simply looked at me until my blood ran cold, never moved an eyelid. We got to within fifteen feet of him; that is, he was that much under us, and he was longer than our canoe, which is eighteen feet. I realised with a start what a damned fool I was and how utterly helpless we were, so cut the line in a real good fright. The last I saw of that shark he was in the same position, looking at me with those eyes of his. It was really quite a time before the hair at the back of my neck went down to its normal position.

We went over to the dredger for the needful which they kindly provided free of cost. Feeling better, we went off towards home, and whilst on the way hooked a tarpon. At the final tiring of this fish there were three attendant sharks, but they just didn't get him, although one had a good try alongside us – so near that I thought he would overturn us.

However, the two men beat the water with their paddles, really in a blue funk, so was I, and Hassan got the tarpon by the gills and heaved him in. One of the sharks followed us in just behind all the way, so my man did not dally that journey.

On landing, I had a good talk to myself about the whole proceedings, and determined that I was every fool under the sun and not to do it again. My nerves wouldn't stand much more of it. I don't mind having two feet on the sand, but that cranky canoe out there was not good enough. For two nights I had the first nightmares of my life as far as I can remember, and shark's eyes formed too large a portion of them for sound sleep.

I took the tarpon to Lagos where it was weighed – eighty pounds. Several fellows came to see it, and one of the doctors told me that the natives catch the same fish at Sierra Leone in nets or hand lines – he had forgotten which. It was not good eating at all, so the boys and their friends polished it off. I am very sorry now I didn't dry the head and keep it for a memento.

That really finished my fishing, which, I think you will admit, was about as exciting as ever we dreamt about in our wildest dreams. I got on to the mail steamer, went round to Forcados, then up the Niger on a Government mail boat without any untold excitement. I shall be here for a short time and then return to my old station, Ibi.

This letter has gone to a most extraordinary length, but I hope you will be interested. I received your letter on spinning for pike, and it did bring back many memories. I shall be returning on leave in November, so it won't be long now before I am fishing the old places with you and Henry.

With kindest regards to you all,

Yours

Oliver.

Hugh Copley, *The Letters of Two Fishermen*, 1930.

The Greatest Salmon of All

No collection of angling stories would be complete without this marvellous and oft-told tale of the British record salmon caught by the gallant Miss Ballantine in 1922 and never beaten.

Saturday, 7 September 1922 started well for Miss Ballantine. In the morning she took three respectable salmon, weighing 17 lb, 21 lb and 25 lb. At dusk on the same day her father, James Ballantine, who was then fisherman for the Laird of Glendelvine, Sir Alexander Lyle, took her out in the boat for an hour's harling, that curious form of fishing indigenous to the Tay and scarcely practised elsewhere. The boatman, in this case James Ballantine, rows back and forth across the current – the Tay is roughly 60 yards wide – skilfully covering salmon lies that have been known and studied for hundreds of years. Sometimes even three rods are set up to trail fly or lure over the stern.

On this evening there were two rods; a split-cane with a Wilkinson fly, and a great heavy greenheart attached to a now obsolete revolving lure of a mottled brown colour called a 'dace'. The weather, Miss B. recalls, was quiet and balmy, as fine an autumn evening as one could wish for.

At 6.15 the dace was taken suddenly and violently. The shock nearly pulled the rod from her hands, but she regained control, keeping the line tight and clear of the other rod. Her father held the boat steady; somehow they managed to get the other rod in and clear the scene for action. At that point she knew, 'there was something very, very heavy on'. The unseen monster led them back and forth across the river in sweeping 50-yard rushes. At one point it slipped behind a rock into a deep lie. Terrified she might lose it, Miss B. kept a tight but delicate control of her line while her father swiftly manoeuvred the boat downstream of the rock to keep the line from rubbing and fraying. Suddenly the fish shot clear, Miss B. kept a tight line and the fish was still hers. Slowly they were towed down river to a point opposite their cottage. They saw Mrs Ballantine on the river-bank, lantern in hand, peering into what was now a pitch-black night. They shouted to her what was happening and followed the fish hoping for even a glimpse of it. But not once did it surface; there was nothing but the great silent weight and the line slicing through the black water.

A hundred yards below the cottage is Caputh Bridge. The bridge has two pilings, and as the boat hugged the left bank of the river their quarry made a determined rush for the far shore. Inevitably the line would be broken. With waning strength Miss B. applied as great a strain as she dared and slowly the fish turned, slipping between the pilings where James Ballantine, rowing frantically, could just follow. She was ready to drop from exhaustion, but her father refused to touch the rod. This was a challenge only she could answer.

It was nearly two hours since the salmon had been hooked in the Boat Pool. Now they were half a mile down the stream. Once more, keeping a tight line, Miss B. reeled in, and felt with aching arms that the creature she had not yet seen was almost ready to be taken. It was moving slowly, in short bursts. Gently she urged it closer to the boat until they could see that the line entered the water almost vertically; somewhere, three or four or five feet down was her fish. Certainly it was ready to be gaffed, but gaffing even a normal-sized fish in the dark is not easy. How were they to manage this leviathan? James inched his way aft, set the gaff against the line and slowly moved it down until he felt the knot of the leader. Had he not made it himself? Did he not know precisely how many blood knots he had made in the expensive silkworm gut? He ran the head of the gaff down into the water, counting each time he felt a tiny protuberance. Three, four, five . . . the fish must be just below. He pushed forward gently, then turned the gaff and drew it up quickly. There was no mistake; with his great strong hands he brought his daughter's catch to the surface and with one big heave, he dragged it over the gunwales. The fish, even after more than two hours, was by no means exhausted, and leaped and flapped in the bottom of the boat. 'Father thought it was going to jump back into the river and threw himself on top of it.' Miss B. sipped her tea, her eyes sparkling. 'My whole arm felt paralysed, and I was so utterly exhausted I could have lain down beside the fish and slept.'

'Well, two men were hailed to carry it slung on a pole to the farm, where it was weighed and witnessed by 16 people.' Many times before the morning she woke with nightmares, and found herself clutching the brass railing of her bedstead as she had clung to the rod that afternoon. Her arms remained swollen for two weeks.

Her name was famous when she woke. Papers throughout Britain carried news of her achievement and every detail of the fish. Weight 64 lb; length 54 in; girth 28 in.

Miss B. said: 'Next day, Sunday, the news went round like wildfire and people came from far and near to see the monster. Our laird, Sir Alexander, sent it to the Perth Royal Infirmary where it went over with both patients and staff. The fun began on Monday when it was taken to Malloch's the tackle shop in Perth. I happened to go round by Scott Street in the afternoon and there was a big crowd around Malloch's window. I thought there had been an accident; instead the fish was displayed in the window with a placard stating its weight and that it had been caught by Miss Ballantine. I went round to the back and stood for a moment beside two old chaps with white side-whiskers. One said to the other 'A woman? Nae woman ever took a fish like that oot of the water mon, I would need a horse, a block and tackle, tae tak a fish like that oot. A woman – that's a lee anyway.' I had a quiet chuckle up my sleeve and ran to catch the bus.

From *The Field*, 1922.

On the Pleasures of Cow Fishing

It must be clearly understood that I am not at all proud of this performance. In Florida men sometimes hook and land, on rod and tackle a little finer than a steam-crane and chain, a mackerel-like fish called 'tarpon' which sometimes run to 120 pounds. Those men stuff their captures and exhibit them in glass cases and become puffed up. On the Columbia River sturgeon of 150 pounds weight are taken with the line. When the sturgeon is hooked the line is fixed to the nearest pine tree or steamboat wharf, and after some hours or days the sturgeon surrenders himself if the pine or line do not give way. The owner of the line then states on oath that he has caught a sturgeon and he too becomes proud.

These things are mentioned to show how light a creel will fill the ordinary man with vanity. I am not proud. It is nothing to me that I have hooked and played several hundred pounds weight of quarry. All my desire is to place the little affair on record before the mists of memory breed the miasma of exaggeration.

The minnow cost eighteenpence. It was a beautiful quill minnow, and the tackle-maker said that it could be thrown as a fly. He guaranteed further in respect to the triangles – it glittered with triangles – that, if necessary, the minnow would hold a horse. A man who speaks too much truth is just as offensive as a man who speaks too little. None the less, owing to the defective condition of the present law of libel, the tackle-maker's name must be withheld.

F i s h   T a l e s

The minnow and I and a rod went down to a brook to attend to a small jack who lived between two clumps of flags in the most cramped swim that he could select. As a proof that my intentions were strictly honourable, I may mention that I was using a light split-cane rod – very dangerous if the line runs through weeds, but very satisfactory in clean water, inasmuch as it keeps a steady strain on the fish and prevents him from taking liberties. I had an old score against the jack. He owed me two live-bait already, and I had reason to suspect him of coming up-stream and interfering with a little bleak-pool under a horse-bridge which lay entirely beyond his sphere of legitimate influence. Observe, therefore, that my tackle and my motives pointed clearly to jack, and jack alone; though I knew that there were monstrous big perch in the brook.

The minnow was thrown as a fly several times, and, owing to my peculiar, and hitherto unpublished, methods of fly throwing, nearly six pennyworth of the triangles came off, either in my coatcollar, or my thumb, or the back of my hand. Fly fishing is a very gory amusement.

The jack was not interested in the minnow, but towards twilight a boy opened a gate of the field and let in some twenty or thirty cows and half-a-dozen cart-horses, and they were all very much interested. The horses galloped up and down the field and shook the banks, but the cows walked solidly and breathed heavily, as people breathe who appreciate the Fine Arts.

By this time I had given up all hope of catching my jack fairly, but I wanted the live-bait and bleak-account settled before I went away, even if I tore up the bottom of the brook. Just before I had quite made up my mind to borrow a tin of chloride of lime from the farm-house – another triangle had fixed itself in my fingers – I made a cast which for pure skill, exact judgement of distance, and perfect coincidence of hand and eye and brain, would have taken every prize at a bait-casting tournament. That was the first half of the cast. The second was postponed because the quill minnow would not return to its proper place, which was under the lobe of my left ear. It had done thus before, and I supposed it was in collision with a grass tuft, till I turned round and saw a large red and white bald faced cow trying to rub what would be withers in a horse with her nose. She looked at me reproachfully, and her look said as plainly as words: 'The season is too far advanced for gadflies. What is this strange disease?'

I replied, 'Madam, I must apologize for an unwarrantable liberty on the part of my minnow, but if you will have the goodness to keep still until I can reel in, we will adjust this little difficulty.'

I reeled in very swiftly and cautiously, but she would not wait. She put her tail in the air and ran away. It was a purely involuntary motion on my part: I struck. Other anglers may contradict me, but I firmly believe that if a man had foul-hooked his best friend through the nose, and that friend ran, the man would strike by instinct. I struck, therefore, and the reel began to sing just as merrily as though I had caught my jack. But had it been a jack, the minnow would have come away. I told the tackle-maker this much afterwards, and he laughed and made allusions to the guarantee about holding a horse.

Because it was a fat innocent she-cow that had done me no harm the minnow held – held like an anchor-fluke in coral moorings – and I was forced to dance up and down an interminable field very largely used by cattle. It was like salmon fishing in a nightmare. I took gigantic strides, and every stride found me up to my knees in marsh. But the cow seemed to skate along the squashy green by the brook, to skim over the miry backwaters and to float like a mist through the patches of rush that squirted black filth over my face. Sometimes we whirled through a mob of her friends – there were no friends to help me – and they looked scandalized; and sometimes a young and frivolous cart-horse would join in the chase for a few miles, and kick pieces of mud into my eyes; and through all the mud, the milky smell of kine, the rush and the smother, I was aware of my own voice crying: 'Pussy, pussy, pussy! Pretty pussy! Come along then, puss-cat!' You see it is so hard to speak to a cow properly, and she would not listen – no, she would not listen.

Then she stopped, and the moon got up behind the pollards to tell the cows to lie down; but they were all on their feet, and they came trooping to see. And she said, 'I haven't had my supper, and I want to go to bed, and please don't worry me.'

And I said, 'The matter has passed beyond any apology. There are three courses open to you, my dear lady. If you'll have the common sense to walk up to my creel I'll get my knife and you shall have all the minnow. Or, again, if you'll let me move across to your near side, instead of keeping me so coldly on your off side, the thing will come away in one tweak. I can't pull it out over your withers. Better still, go to a post and rub it out, dear. It won't hurt much, but if you think I'm going to lose my rod to please you, you are mistaken.'

And she said, 'I don't understand what you are saying. I am very, very unhappy.'

And I said, 'It's all your fault for trying to fish. Do go to the nearest gatepost, you nice fat thing, and rub it out.'

For a moment I fancied she was taking my advice. She ran away and I followed. But all the other cows came with us in a bunch, and I thought of Phaeton trying to drive the Chariot of the Sun, and Texan cowboys killed by stampeding cattle, and 'Green Grow the Rushes, Oh' and Solomon and Job, and 'loosing the bands of Orion', and hooking Behemoth, and Wordsworth who talks about whirling round with stones and rocks and trees, and 'Here we go round the Mulberry Bush', and 'Pippin Hill', and 'Hey Diddle Diddle', and most especially the top joint of my rod. Again she stopped – but nowhere in the neighbourhood of my knife – and her sisters stood moonfaced round her. It seemed that she might, now, run towards me, and I looked for a tree, because cows are very different from salmon, who only jump against the line, and never molest the fisherman. What followed was worse than any direct attack. She began to buckjump, to stand on her head and her tail alternately, to leap into the sky, all four feet together, and to dance on her hind legs. It was so violent and improper, so desperately unladylike, that I was inclined to blush, as one would blush at the sight of a prominent statesman sliding down a fire escape, or a duchess chasing her cook with a skillet. That flopsome abandon might go on all night in the lonely meadow among the mists, and if it went on all night – this was pure inspiration – I might be able to worry through the fishing line with my teeth.

Those who desire an entirely new sensation should chew with all their teeth, and against time, through a best waterproofed silk line, one end of which belongs to a mad cow dancing fairy rings in the moonlight; at the same time keeping one eye on the cow and the other on the top joint of a split-cane rod. She buckjumped and I bit on the slack just in front of the reel; and I am in a position to state that that line was cored with steel wire throughout the particular section which I attacked. This has been formally denied by the tackle-maker, who is not to be believed.

Fish Tales

The wheep of the broken line running through the rings told me that henceforth the cow and I might be strangers. I had already bidden good-bye to some tooth or teeth; but no price is too great for freedom of the soul.

'Madam', I said, 'the minnow and twenty feet of very superior line are your alimony without reservation. For the wrong I have unwittingly done to you I express my sincere regret. At the same time, may I hope that Nature, the kindest of nurses, will in due season.' She or one of her companions must have stepped on her spare end of the line in the dark, for she bellowed wildly and ran away, followed by all the cows. I hoped the minnow was disengaged at last; and before I went away looked at my watch, fearing to find it nearly midnight. My last cast for the jack was made at 6.23 p.m. There lacked still three and a-half minutes of the half-hour; and I would have sworn that the moon was paling before the dawn.

'Simminly someone were chasing they cows down to bottom o' Ten Acre,' said the farmer that evening. ''Twasn't you, sir?'

'Now under what earthly circumstances do you suppose I should chase your cows? I wasn't fishing for them, was I?'

Then all the farmer's family gave themselves up to jam-smeared laughter for the rest of the evening, because that was a rare and precious jest, and it was repeated for months, and the fame of it spread from that farm to another, and yet another at least three miles away, and it will be used again for the benefit of visitors when the freshets come down in spring.

But to the greater establishment of my honour and glory I submit in print this bald statement of fact, that I may not, through forgetfulness, be tempted later to tell how I hooked a bull on a Marlow Buzz, how he ran up a tree and took to water, and how I played him along the London-road for thirty miles, and gaffed him at Smithfields. Errors of this kind may creep in with the lapse of years, and it is my ambition ever to be a worthy member of that fraternity who pride themselves on never deviating by one hair's breadth from the absolute and literal truth.

Rudyard Kipling, *Short Stories*, 1910.

Fish Tales

A Fish from Logie's Linn

Here is another wonderful piece from the immortal pen of Patrick Chalmers, whose gift for comic writing was as great as his gift for characterization, dialogue and drama.

There was once a young man in a shooting-lodge among the misty red hills and it was Lammas time. And the rain roared and hammered on rood and windows and, on such a day as yon, you would not be driving a grouse were it ever so. And the young man could not play at bridge for he had not the bridge faculty. But neither had he a fishing-rod, for he had come to shoot grouse and not to catch burn trouts. So he stood in the window and listened to the singing of the showers. And he went to the hall door and opened it, and the West Wind, sweet with the rain and the smell of the pinewoods, went by with a shout and bade him follow it. It was then that his host told that, if a body walked two miles over the hill, that he would come to the Logie Water wherein were trout for the catching. The rod to take them on was still the difficulty. But a rod was borrowed from the bothy. It was a little old two-piece trout-rod and it was lashed with binding and bound about with twine. But it was light and whippy and the handicraft of a great maker of old, and Peter Stuart had had it 'in a present' from 'her leddyship' at Druim this long time ago.

But the young man was not concerned for the genesis of the rod so long as he might get a loan of it. And to this he was kindly welcome. There was a sufficiency of line on the reel too. And, as it passed the not too drastic testing of a line, all was well. Peter had some baithooks and a yard or two of gut. The procuring of a 'pucklie' worms, in wet moss and a mustard-tin, would not hinder long. And so the guest was provided for. And presently he swung a game-bag upon his back, for creel there was none, and, syne, he was for away. But not before he had remembered that, in the cap to match with his Lovat mixture of yesterday's wearing, there were two or three trout-flies. So it was that cap that he would put on. And before he did so he asked about the Logie Water, for he knew it not.

The Logie was, it appeared, a wee stony water on most days and the trout that lived in it were wee trout. About six to the pound? They would be just about that, said the angler's host. But they were plump and golden little trout and dusted on with crimson spots, and sometimes, maybe, there was a half-pounder to be had. The Logie ran into the Waupie of course. And the Waupie was a salmon river? Why, yes, the Waupie was a salmon river, but no salmon were ever in the Logie because they could not get up the Linn of Logie. And a very good reason too, thought the angler as he crossed the hill. And the West Wind was blowing steady and the rain was going out on it. But the hills were full of the roar of waters where the burns ran foaming full. And the mist rose out of the glens and the corries and shifted, like grey smoke, and through it the hills, what a man might see of them, were very dark and blue. And when the angler got to the Logie Water he thought that it was a real bonny little river.

Like all the hill waters the Logie rose like a rocket. But she cleared soon and then she ran in good and swirling ply for a whole fishing day before she fell in and went trickling among the humpbacked stones that huddled in the course of her like a herd of sheep that lie in a park. But there were none of these river-sheep to show to-day. A sleek back here and a sleek back there perhaps, a swirl, a curl, a brown eddy to mark, you'd say, a likely cast, a likely resting place for a running fish. That is, did salmon run the Logie. But no salmon ever ran the Logie because none, as we know, may mount the Linn of Logie. Which was a sad pity, said the angler, for it is a pretty little river, this Logie, and if he, the angler, were Lord Pittenweem, his host's landlord, he'd have the Linn, and the rocks that made it roar, dynamited out of that and a passage made for my lord the salmon.

'This is no worm water, anyhow,' thought the fisherman. And he sat down and considered the flies that he wore in his bonnet. There, tied on gut, were a male March brown, a red palmer, two teals-and-red, and a couple more that he could put no name to. 'They'll serve,' said he, 'and if I fish them single they'll see me through the day.' So our angler took the worms out of the mustard-tin and howked a hole and buried them, moss and all; for he was a young man solicitous of all living things. He mounted the March brown, the March brown that kills well everywhere and, in spite of its specialist title, all the year round.

As he makes his first cast, a slant of sun kisses the water simultaneously with his March brown, and an ouzel speeds upstream and under the angler's very line. The angler notes the pucker where the March brown alights on the Logie Water, and almost before that miniature ring has disappeared there is a flash of

gold at the fly. The angler twitches the rod-top, but the trout has missed the
March brown. To the repeated cast the fingerling responds with a dash and,
hooking himself, tears, for all that he weighs scarce the poor quarter of a
pound, a goodly yard of line off a stiffish reel. He is beached (for the angler has
never a net) where the Logie, fringed with a lace of foam, sweeps round a tiny
curve of sand and small gravel.

The report on the trouts of the Logie has been a true report. This is a
remarkable pretty trout, fat and well-liking, high in the shoulder, deep in the
golden flank and dotted upon, as it was said that he would be, in crimson dots.
So, with a quick tap on his head, the *coup de grace* that every takeable trout
should get ere he be basketed, the game-bag receives him to lie upon two hand-
fuls of hill grass and heather. He is not long alone there for, to the next cast,
there is a glancing rise and a trout that might be the twin of the first is making
'her leddyship's' little rod bend and curtsey as he leaps and leaps again. A game
and a gallant little fighter he is, but in a minute or so he also is drawn up on to
the little circle of sand and his troubles, if ever he had any until now, are over.

The sun is hot by this time and the wet heather is steaming in the kindliness
of light and day. The angler can hear the pop of guns somewhere over the
march. The tenant of Waupie Lodge has evidently gone to the hill for an after-
luncheon hour or two. But our friend is very well content to be where he is.
The little Logie trout are worth a lot of grouse and, moreover, none so little as
all that are some of them. For on the edge of a smooth break, a streaming swirl
that marks the sunken boulder, Troll-tossed a million years ago from a mountain top to lie for all time in Logie as the shelter of great trout, the March
brown is taken with a devil of a tug. And almost before the angler can raise the
point of 'her Leddyship', for, as such, he has come to know lovingly the little
engine at his command, a great trout, every ounce of three-quarters of a pound,
fat as butter, golden as guineas, leaps with a shattering leap and, falling with a
splash, has gone and the March brown with him.

Well now, that's a pity and all, but there are over two dozen trout in the
game-bag and an uncommon pretty creel they are and uncommon well, no
doubt, they will taste, split and fried and eaten with cold fresh butter and a
sprig of parsley. And talking of eating it is now three-thirty and the angler has
not yet eaten the egg sandwiches that Maggie came running after him with as

he went out. He will eat them now therefore. And that done, shall it be the Palmer as a second horse, or one of the anonymous insects – or a teal-and-red.

A teal-and-red it is, and now the angler will catch another five trouts to make the three dozen and then be facing the lodge-ward two miles up along the march burn, over the rigging, down hill again, and so home. This pool is a real picture of a pool and it is a thousand sorrows that salmon cannot loup the Linn of Logie, for, if they could, you'd say, in this water, that it is here you'd get into a fish. The river shoots and tumbles in peacock tails of amber, over an upheaval of granite it goes, with a flounce of foam, and so, into a deep, fast, porter-coloured pool – a pool that thins out on to a wide shallow of gravel that, in turn, contracts into the rough-and-tumble neck of another important-looking piece of water.

Very quickly the angler catches a further three of the game little trout to whom he has grown accustomed. And the teal-and-red now explores the glassy honey-coloured glide, the fan of clearing water, and it all happens in a second of time, there is a welt of sudden silver that shoots athwart just where the teal-and-red – ah, no salmon can loup – but 'her Leddyship's' slight nose is pulled, for all that, most savagely a-down and the line goes off the stiff reel with a shriek.

Twenty yards out and the hooked fish, finding the shallow, throws himself sideways out of the water, clean and beautiful and swift, the salmon who has louped the Linn – the sea-silver salmon who has established a precedent! And back he comes into the dark water with a dash that takes him upstream, up till almost he'd leave the pool at the top of it. Indeed, for a moment he hangs in the very tumult of the entry, then as the angler comes opposite to him, he goes down, down under the boughs of the birks on the far bank and the line buzzing like bees.

Splash, he is on the shallow once more. He jolts and he lunges, and then 'her Leddyship' is pulled almost straight as the rough water at the neck of the next pool takes charge of the fish. Headlong down he goes and headlong the angler follows after him – fifty dividing yards after him, fifty of the sixty yards of line that the reel runs to. The next pool is a bonny pool too – bonny from an artistic point of view anyhow – but rock-staked and swirling, a bad place to beat a fish in. And beaten he must be, for at the tail of this pool boils the Linn itself and plunges over and down in spouts of waterfalls. However, there is seventy yards of water to go or ever the fish may make the fall, and half-way thereto is a bit of shelving gravel and backwater which the angler notes well. The fish, six pounds is he, eight perhaps, has had a rattling and if he can be brought to the gravel the rod shall do yet. And so 'her Leddyship' bends and condescends with all her slim might.

And gradually the fish comes to her, heavily now and sometimes with the wedge of his steel-grey tail cutting the surface. The angler holds him as tightly as he dares, gives him such of the butt as he presumes. And the gods are on his side, for, rolling this way and that way, the fish comes to hand. And the angler, with a last guiding pressure, lays him, head and shoulders, on the beach, and dropping 'her Leddyship', he tails the only salmon that ever louped Logie's Linn.

Patrick Chalmers, *The Linn of Logie*, 1931.

A Pike from the Squire's

Francis Francis was one of the great fishing authorities of the Victorian era. He wrote several books including The Art of Angling *(1867), and* Sporting Sketches, *from which this extract is taken.*

Dear J., – I've got a day on Lord Thompson's water for self and friend. I mean to go the first open day in February, so rig out some big live snaps and watch the weather. I'll take the lunch, and I will leave the drinks and baits to you. Thine Piscatorially . . .

Thus I wrote, some years ago, to my friend J., a slayer of mighty pike, indeed, his friends call him 'Jack-the-Giant killer'. Now, I am not going to tell you where Lord Thompson's water is – old pike fishers keep these things to themselves; and you need not look for Lord Thompson's name in the peerage, and so on to his country seat, because it isn't in it, and I shan't give what old

On the way to fish, by W.D. Sadler

F i s h   T a l e s

Nicholas used to call 'my sportive readers' a chance to mob Lord T. with letters for asking permission. The cheek and perseverance of the London pike fisher in pursuit of permissions for his recreation is unbounded; and the ingenious multiplicity of pleas which he will put in to a perfect stranger, of whom he knows nothing save that he has some pike fishing, is wonderful. Old D., the well-known cricketer, was a desperate hand at ferreting out permissions; but he got a rebuff once, which made him look all round the compass, and wonder whether he was D. or someone else who had been 'stumped' for a 'duck's egg'. There was a grand match on at Lord's, and old Squire L. of L. always attended all the matches at Lord's. D. happened to hear that he had about the best pike fishing in the Kingdom, but was rather 'sticky' in giving orders; but thinking that when he got him well on in a chat over his favourite pastime he might slip in a request for a day, he laid his plans accordingly. The stumps were set; the match about to begin; old D. on the look out. When he saw the Squire drive up four-in-hand and enter the ground, D. carefully meandered round till he came upon him.

'Ah, D.! What sort of a match shall we have today?' and the conversation began; and D., who as a rule was a most disputatious cantankerous man, was highly deferential. The Squire was jolly chatty, and D. saw that day's fishing coming nearer and nearer. At length he made a dash for it.

'I hear, Squire, that you have some good pike fishing at L. I should like to try my luck there very much if you would allow me.'

I have said the squire was 'sticky' in giving permission, but 'sticky' is not the word. He never gave permission at all save under very unusual circumstances. He hated to give leave; he didn't fish himself, but he couldn't abide to see any one else fishing. His countenance changed.

'I keep my fishing for my friends, Mr D.,' said the squire, frigidly, and with emphasis on the 'friends' and the 'mister' – 'and you're not one of them – good morning,' and off went the squire to back old D.'s tip, while D. said something naughty under his breath, and wished he had the squire before the wicket and without pads on.

Time went over; February set in mild but not too warm and sunny. The day was fixed; the morning came. An early repast of sausages, ham, toast, coffee, eggs, and marmalade, put me in fettle; a large luncheon basket, duly stuffed with varieties, another basket with sundries, a large double hand rush basket and a pair of rods made my outfit when I met J. at the Knockemdown station on the Pick-me-up-in-pieces line. J. was tremendously picturesque, and what with kettles, &c., &c., we looked like Robinson Crusoe and his man Friday in pursuit of the savages. J. was a prodigious smoker, and he had a bowsprit in the shape of a Regalia Elephanta about a foot or so long.

'Standard! Telegraph!'

'Here, boy, give us both,' and in five minutes J. was deep in the markets, and I was in the telegrams, as we sped on to our destination. At Bunkemout junction we found a trap waiting. A drive of three miles brought us to the keeper's cottage, a paradise of woodbine, china roses, &c., in the summer, and pretty enough even now. Alfred was waiting for us, and getting the cans and baskets led the way down through a sunken lane with high sandy banks, across a field to a line of pollards, and there we were. It was a lovely backwater with a stage of bucks in the middle of it, and looked, as J. said, 'doosedly like pike'. There were holes and long eddies and shallows, with rushes and reeds here and there, and a proper complement of stubs and piles, of course put there on purpose to lose fish.

'Well, Alfred, got any fish for us today?'

'There be plenty there if you can catch 'em, sir. There's one as I do wish you may; he's the biggest I've sin here this many a day; he've yeat a hull brood o' ducks wi' the down for stuffin', drat 'im.'

'What'll he weigh, Alfred?'

'He'll goo ower thirty pound, sir. He mostly lies in that long deep eddy by the pollards, just above the bucks, which is the wust thing in the way as can be; but there's plenty good ones aside he; we allus has 'em here when there's a flood, and the big flood last month have stocked us finely. I think we'll put all the things we don't want to use under the wall by the bucks yanner,' and he did so.

'I shall spin this lower reach below the bucks down, I think, J., unless you prefer to.'

'No, I'll put on a live snap, and try the pool above the bucks,' said J., and the rods being soon together, the tackle fixed, and the baits on, I turned down stream and began. It was rather more streamy below the bucks, and that was

why I chose spinning. I had, too, a recollection of a good fish I had lost formerly near a willow stump half way down, and good fish have a knack of always
occupying a good lair. I had a Chapman spinner – one of Woods' pattern. It
saves a lot of trouble – preserves the bait, and always spins fairly – and, as your
tail triangle flies loose, it does not miss many fish. I now generally carry three
or four of different sizes to suit the baits and the fish, and in five minutes thirty
yards of line were flying across the water. '

I don't mean to brag, but I learnt of the best master on the Thames, have
practised a great deal, and think I do it pretty well. Across the stream with a
slight splash, just to attract the fish's notice, and the bait comes spinning and
whirling round in a seductive curve, as if it were going round a ball room in
the Walpurgis Waltz. Once more the line is gathered in; a slight heave and a
swing, and away flies the bait again, and along it comes like a streak of silver.
The third time, as I was watching it, I saw a slight ridge in the water, and the
bait seemed to disappear. There was a check, followed by 'sshuck' from me, and
I let him have it smartly. 'Whizz' and out went a dozen yards of line. One
doesn't part with much, as a rule, to a pike; but this fellow, being in a stream,
was a lively chap, and made a strong fight of it before I could get him near
Alfred's landing net; but at length he got near enough, the net slipped under
him, and out he came, a handsome six-pound fish, like a green tiger, and kicking like old Joe.

'Hi, hi, hi!' from J. broke in here.

'Run to Mr J. with the net; he's in a tidy fish by the bend of his rod,' and
Alfred sped away, while I straightened the dace on my Chapman, it being little
damaged.

There seemed to be a little more difficulty with J.'s fish than mine, which
was accounted for when Alfred came back with the intelligence that J. had broken his ice with a good ten-pounder.

Away flew my bait again clean across the water, dropping with a slight
splash just clear of the opposite bushes. Half a dozen casts, and I saw a bulge in
the water of a good fish following, but he shied off and didn't take. Another
cast, but he didn't take, so I left him.

'That's a tidy fish there, sir. I see him t'other day just under that bush. He'll
go a dozen pounds when you get him out.' But as he didn't take I marked him

down, and went on a few yards lower down, where I turned over a fair fish, but he was away directly. I cast again instantly to the spot without a second's delay, and he came like a lion at it, and I had him, but only for a moment or two, for once more he got off, and this time he had had enough of me. He seemed to be a nice fish of 7 lb, or thereabouts. My bait being rather done up now, I put on a new one, and while I was doing so, 'Hi, hi, hi!' came down the bank, and away went Alfred to assist J. in landing a five-pounder, while I spun on for twenty or thirty yards without a touch.

Alfred had returned, and was relating to me the incidents of the last course, when in mid-stream I got a heavy pull, and, giving the fish a severe 'rugg', I was soon at the old game again. Up stream he went, and then up again, and then, like a salmon, he made two leaps into the air, falling back with a bang, and showing inches which seemed about the counterpart of the last fish, and brought my heart into my mouth. Fortunately, the hooks held, although he rather alarmed me into the prevalent notion that he was lightly hooked in consequence of his jumping; but it was not so, he was well hooked, only the flying tail hooks had caught him outside near the eye, poor beast! After ten or twelve minutes, I repeat, Alfred managed to spoon him out, and having earned it, I lighted a weed, and thought the day was hopeful. After this I got a nice little fish of 4 lb, which was the lowest size allowed, but, resolved to do the liberal thing, I turned him in again, as I did a three-pounder just after. Then there was another 'Hi, hi, hi!' from J., and once more Alfred made tracks, and assisted in the landing of an eight-pounder.

I still worked on down towards the willow tree I mentioned. The stump projected out over the water, and there was a deep hole under it, any fisherman would spot it for a good fish; halfway across the stream the hole shallowed up to about three or four feet deep. 'Now, carefully, carefully', and seeing that my bait spun well, and that all was clear, I sent it careering across the shallow and brought it whirling round the hole, 'heave and pull, heave and pull'. It works into a straight line just below the stump, and comes darting past the stump. 'Now or never.'

'Confound the fish, he's either not at home or not hungry.'

'I see him feeding on the shaller and makin' the baits fly, rarely,' said Alfred, 'and I judge he's a 17 lb or 18 lb fish; I've seed him many times.'

Round came the bait again, but no result followed.

'Not today, Alfred,' I said, as I turned round to get below the tree.

At that moment there was a loud splash – a deuce of a tug at my rod point, and as the rod was firmly over my shoulder, he got it pretty hot; nevertheless, to make sure I gave him another rugg. The bait was just hanging on the water, turning lazily round on the surface, as the stream caught the fans, and the temptation was too much for him, so he rose like a salmon at a fly, and took it, and I held him. Down he dashed to the very end of the hole, then out of it, on to the shallow, where he made fine play among the small fry, then back and into the hole again. 'He'll be making for his holt presently, sir,' said Alfred, 'can't you lean down and pass the rod under the tree to me, so as to get below it, and keep him away. If he works up and bolts in under your feet you can't help it; and what old roots and snags there is there Lord only knows.' At the risk of a ducking, and hanging on to the tree by one arm and my eyelids, I passed the rod under, so that Alfred got hold of it by the middle joint. The reel went two feet under water when I let go; but Alfred soon got a tight line on the fish again, which was grubbing along under the bank, and having recovered the rod I hurried down below, and putting a good strain on, brought him away from danger down stream again; and after a little more than a quarter of an hour's tussle, I worked him in on the shallow below where Alfred stood knee deep with the net, and in another minute we had him out, a fine male fish of 16 lb. We regarded him with satisfaction, and drank his health, and so forth. While we had been busy with him, sundry 'hi, hi, hi's!' came down the bank, but, as they could not be attended to, J. was left to his own devices, as he had a pocket gaff. Alfred now went to him. He had hooked a good fish of a dozen pounds or so, played him home, and scratched him severely with the gaff, without hooking him, so the fish got off. Just as Alfred came up he hooked and landed a five-pounder, which he returned, and then another, which was equally lucky.

I went on, and spun the rest of the water down to the bottom for a good hundred yards, but only got hold of one or two small fish. I then went up and tried the fish I had marked down. He came and pulled at me, but very cautiously, so I missed him. As we had breakfasted early, it was pretty well luncheon time, so I shouldered my rod and walked up the bucks, where Alfred was engaged in lighting a fire. My sundry basket produced a fire pot, kettle, saucepan, &c. The luncheon basket turned out a big basin full of jelly, which being turned into the saucepan soon resolved itself into about three pints of fine mock-turtle soup. A shout brought J. upon the scene, who flavoured the soup with a bottle of old East India sherry, and a bottle of very choice Irroy. How we did enjoy that soup. The day was not by any means warm, and we sat in a triangle round the fire, and swallowed a couple of platefuls each. A cold duck was then reduced to bones, and then, in fear the sherry and fizz should not mix properly, I produced a bottle labelled 'cognac' and '1834', and the kettle being now in full sing, we had just one glass of steaming hot grog. 'What's that you say? It was a shame to mix it' – well, perhaps – but after all *que voulez vous?* The best brandy makes the best grog, and if any one manes to deny that proposhition let him just put the print of his big ugly fut on the tail of me coat; whooroo! A comforting pipe, and then we fell to it again. I won't describe the capture of each fish seriatim. I got four more 6 lb, 7 lb, 10 lb, and 11 lb. J. got two of 8 lb and 9 lb, and lost the sockdolager, and we threw in some seven or eight small ones. About one hundred yards above the bucks the cut narrowed and grew deep – twenty yards above was an old pile or two, part of some broken down framework. J. was about to pitch his bait out into the middle of this cut, which he had not yet fished, when Alfred brought him in the landing net a small Jack about ten or eleven inches long which he had just spooned out of a ditch close by.

'Put him on, sir, put him on,' said Alfred. 'If there's ever a whopper handy he's bound to fetch him.'

'But he's too large for my hooks, Alfred. What shall I do?'

'Never mind, sir. If a fish takes it give him plenty o' time and let him gorge. I'll forgive ye if ye kills a little 'un; but ye wun't.'

Thus assured, J. put the fish on somehow, and, pitching it out with a tremendous splash into the very middle of the cut, waited the event. Of course the float went down at once. 'Ain't the bait strong? That's 'ow I likes to see 'em; and don't he keep the float down? Just tighten the line or he'll be getting foul o' weeds.' J. did so, and there was a fierce jag at the rod point.

F i s h   T a l e s

'Why, that ain't the bait; something's took the bait already,' said J., quite excited, as the line began to cut the water slowly, the fish moving up towards a big bank of weeds and rushes about twenty yards above.

'That's the big 'un, for a million. I see him lay there at the tail o' them weeds once or twice last week; he must 'a took it as soon as ever it fell in the water. Give him plenty o' time sir, plenty. Don't worry him whatever you doo's. Let 'n get the 'ooks well in his gullet. Eat my ducks will 'e, ye ould varmint? Jest you swaller that nice little great-great-grandson o' yourn, that's all'; and the fish evidently meant to, for he laid up at the tail of the weeds quietly pouching for nearly a quarter of an hour, while J. stood watching, all of a twitter.

Presently the fish showed an inclination to move, and as he was coming out from his lair into the cut J. let him have it. The stroke was a shrewd one and hurt, for the pike made one dart clean through the reed and rush bed, mowing them down as if with a scythe. Fortunately, J.'s line was stout and new, and the tackle stood it. When he came out into the stream, he made tracks rather, and took out forty or fifty yards of line at a dash; but the stream was pretty clear, the tackle sound, and the hold certain – at least, as Alfred said, 'he'll turn hisself inside out afore he gets rid of them hooks.' Then he began dropping down the cut with a short dash and a heavy drag, every now and then towards the bucks, which were seventy or eighty yards below.

'Drat 'im; take care ye doesn't lev'n get near the bucks, or he'll break ye on them piles as sure as fate, for they're full o' rusty old nails.'

J. did his best, and fought a good fight, but five and thirty pounds is five and thirty pounds, and you can't do as you like with it. The fish was obstinate, and meant going for the bucks; and, in spite of every dodge – in spite of dashing, splashing, stoning to frighten him up again – he merely sheered over to the other side and kept on.

J.'s eyes were half out of his head with indignation at the pike's base behaviour. He'd 'pay him; hang him!'

'Yes, I'm afraid you will; and you won't get through after all. I never saw such a dour headed beast – he's as obstinate as a mule. But he's an awful big 'un,' I said, as J. laid the rod well on, and actually checked the fish for a moment, till the big brute fairly lashed the water into foam as he tumbled and walloped on the surface. The next moment, however, he was away again forty miles an hour down to the bucks.

'I'll pay him. D – n his picture,' said J., panting after. 'By Gad! he'll beat me after all; he's got into the stream that sets for these piles, and I can no more stop him than fly. I'll smash the rod. I'll . . . .'

But the next minute the line grated across the outer pile. There was a plunge and a dash; the rod straightened; the line floated like a pennant in the wind; and J. collapsed.

'Never mind, old man. Take a drop of '34, and never say die. You fought him splendidly, and had the water been clear you must have killed him.'

'Forty pound if he was an ounce,' said J. in a hoarse whisper, as he accepted the flask. 'Getting that way, at any rate, though hardly in the fours.'

Still J. lamented and wouldn't be comforted. 'If he'd only killed that fish.'

'What odds will you lay, old man, you haven't killed him?'

'Bet you a new hat.'

'Done with you. You'll have that fish within a week. Remember there's a float to him with a double hitch, and unless he can jam that very hard some-where he can't break it, but it will hang up every where and wring his soul out. You'll have him in less than a week.' And so he had, for three days after a parcel about four or five feet long, done up in straw, reached the office directed to him, and when he opened it it was the pike, with his own gimp and float, and about four or five yards of line hanging from his mouth. Alfred found the float in the water near the bucks; he got hold of it, and found the fish utterly done, and with little trouble got him ashore, rather wasted, poor beast! He was hooked in the gullet; and even then he weighed 35 lb. Our great taxidermist Cooper set him up gorgeously, and he is the pride of J.'s ancestral halls.

This fight about finished the day. It was then about half-past four, and we didn't care to fish after. So we collected the spoil, we re-kindled the fire, and sat round it for half an hour or so and punished the '34, till the fly was due.

The fish made a brave show. There was exactly a dozen of them: a 5, two 6's, two 7's, two 8's, one 9, two 10's, one 11, and my 16, or over 100 lb weight. Besides this we threw back over a dozen more of three or four pounders; and that shan't be a bad day.

Francis Francis, *Sporting Sketches*, 1890.

Fish Tales

The Death of Two Friends

Guy de Maupassant was one of the great French nineteenth-century novelists. A keen fisherman himself, he occasionally wove a backcloth of fish and fishing into his stories. Here angling is used to heighten the shocking contrast between the peaceful and the murderous.

Paris was blockaded, starving, in the throes of death. The sparrows were becoming scarce on the rooftops and the sewers' population low: people ate whatever they could find. On a bright morning in January, Mr Morissot, a watchmaker by trade and stay-at-home on occasion, was walking along the boulevard, sad, hungry, with his hands in the pockets of his uniform trousers, when he came face to face with a fellow tradesman whom he recognised as a friend. It was Mr Sauvage, a riverside acquaintance.

Every Sunday, before the war, Morissot would leave at daybreak with a fishing rod in one hand and a tin box on his back. He would take the train to Colombes and walk from there to the Isle of Marante, the place of his dreams, where he would immediately start fishing and carry on until dark.

Every Sunday he would meet there a dumpy little man, Mr Sauvage, who kept a haberdasher's shop in the Rue Notre-Damede Lorette, a jovial fellow and, like himself, passionately fond of fishing. They would often spend half a day side by side, fishing rod in hand, feet dangling, and had grown to be friends.

Some days they wouldn't say a word. Sometimes they chatted; but they understood each other without speaking, sharing similar tastes and identical feelings.

On spring mornings at about ten o'clock, when the young sun brought to the surface of the river that thin mist which flows with the current, and poured the pleasant warmth of the new season down the backs of the two keen fishermen, Morissot would sometimes say, 'How delightful!' and Mr Sauvage would answer, 'There's nothing like it!' and that was enough: they understood and respected each other.

On autumn evenings, when the setting sun turned the sky blood-red, throwing scarlet reflections on to the water, setting the horizon ablaze, enveloping

74

the two friends in a fiery glow and pouring gold on the already rust-coloured trees, Mr Sauvage would look at Morissot and say with a smile, 'What a grand sight!' 'It beats the boulevard, doesn't it?' Morissot would answer, filled with wonder, without taking his eyes off his float.

As soon as they had recognised each other they shook hands warmly, greatly excited at meeting under such different circumstances. 'What terrible events!' sighed Mr Sauvage. 'And what weather!' groaned Morissot sadly. 'This is the first nice day we have had this year.'

The sky was indeed clear and blue.

They started walking side by side, dreamy and sad. Morissot went on, 'Do you remember our fishing expeditions? How nice they were!'

'Shall we ever go again?' asked Mr Sauvage.

They went into a little cafe, had a glass of absinthe and then resumed their walk. Morissot suddenly stopped. 'What about another drink?' Mr Sauvage agreed and they went into another cafe.

When they came out again they felt quite dizzy, light-headed, as one does after drinking alcohol on an empty stomach. It was a mild day. A soft breeze caressed their faces. The balmy air made the drinks go to Mr Sauvage's head. He stopped and said,

'Suppose we go?'

'Where?'

'Fishing.'

'Fishing! Where?'

'To our island, of course. The French soldiers are stationed near Colombes. I know Colonel Dumoulin; they'll let us through.'

Morissot quivered with anticipation. 'All right; count me in.' And they parted to fetch their fishing tackle.

An hour later they were walking side by side along the main road. They soon reached the villa the Colonel occupied. He smiled at their request and agreed to satisfy their whim. Off they set again with a pass. They soon crossed the outposts, walked through a deserted Colombes and found themselves at the edge of the small vineyards which slope down to the Seine. It was about eleven o'clock.

Opposite, the village of Argenteuil looked dead. The heights of Orgemont and Sannois dominated the whole area. The vast plain, with its bare cherry trees and grey expanse of ground, stretching as far as Nanterre, was quite empty. 'The Prussians are up there,' Mr Sauvage whispered, pointing to the top. Fear paralysed the two friends as they surveyed the deserted area.

'The Prussians!' They had never seen any, but they had been conscious of their presence around Paris for months, destroying, pillaging, massacring, starving France, invisible and all-powerful. This added a kind of superstitious terror to the heat they felt towards this unknown and victorious people.

'What if we meet any?' stammered Morissot.

'We'll offer them some fish!' Mr Sauvage answered, his Parisian banter coming to the surface in spite of everything.

But they were reluctant to venture into the countryside; the silence frightened them. Mr Sauvage finally made up his mind: 'Come on, let's go. But carefully!' and they made their way down into a vineyard, bent double, crawling, taking cover behind every bush, looking and listening tensely.

An exposed strip of land had to be crossed to get to the river. They started to run; as soon as they reached the bank they sank into the dry reeds.

Morissot put his ear to the ground to listen for footsteps. He heard nothing; they were alone, quite alone.

Reassured, they started to fish.

Opposite, the deserted Isle of Marante prevented them from being seen from the other bank. The little restaurant was shut up, it looked as if it had been abandoned years ago. Mr Sauvage caught the first fish, Morissot the second, and every minute up came their lines with a little silvery fish wriggling on the ends of them – they were miraculously lucky.

Gently they slipped the fish into a fine-mesh keep-net which lay in the water at their feet. They were filled with delight, the delight which one feels on taking up a pleasant pastime again after having been deprived of it for a long time.

The kindly sun poured its warmth between their shoulders. They were no longer listening for anything, nor thinking of anything. The rest of the world was forgotten; they were fishing.

But suddenly they heard a muffled sound which seemed to come from underground, making the earth shake. The cannon had started booming again.

Morissot looked round and over the bank to the left he could see in the distance the tall outline of Mont Valerien bearing a white plume on its brow, a mist of powder which it had just spat out.

Then, straight away, another jet of smoke came from the top of the fortress, and a few moments later another explosion.

Others followed, and every minute the mountain exhaled its ominous breath and blew forth its milky vapour, which rose slowly against the peaceful sky, forming a cloud above it.

'Here they go again,' said Mr Sauvage, shrugging his shoulders.

Mr Morissot was a peace-loving man and as he watched the feather on his float dip twice in succession, anger suddenly seized him at the thought of these madmen who were fighting there.

'They must be daft to kill each other like that,' he grumbled.

'Worse than animals,' continued Mr Sauvage.

And Morissot, who had just caught a bleak, declared, 'And to think that it will always be like that as long as there are governments.'

Mr Sauvage cut in, 'The Republicans wouldn't have declared war . . .'

Morissot interrupted him: 'With a king you have war outside, with a republic inside.' And quietly they started to discuss great political problems with the sound reasoning of simple, peaceable men, both agreeing on one point – there was no freedom to be had. And Mont Valerien went on booming ceaselessly, demolishing French houses with its cannonballs, crushing lives, putting an end to many a dream, to many expected joys and hoped for happiness, bringing suffering to the hearts of women, girls, and mothers far away in other countries, suffering which would never end.

'That's life,' declared Mr Sauvage.

'You mean death!' said Morissot, laughing.

Suddenly they started – someone was walking behind them. They turned and saw four men standing right behind them, four tall, bearded men dressed like servants in livery with flat caps on their heads, and pointing rifles right at them.

They both dropped their fishing rods which floated away down the river.

In a few seconds they were caught, bound, dragged off and thrown into a boat which the soldiers then rowed across to the island.

Fish Tales

Behind the house which the two friends had thought to be deserted, they saw a score of Prussian soldiers.

A kind of hairy giant who was sitting astride a chair smoking a big porcelain pipe, asked them in excellent French, 'Well, gentlemen, how was the fishing?'

Just then a soldier deposited at the officer's feet the net full of fish which he had taken care to bring along.

The Prussian smiled. 'Ah! I see it was going rather well, but that's not the point. Listen to me and don't panic.'

'As far as I am concerned, you are two spies sent to watch me. I have captured you and will shoot you. You were pretending to fish as a cover to your real purpose. You fell into my hands; bad luck – war is war. But as you came past the outposts, you must have had the password to get through. Give it to me and you can go free.'

The two friends stood side by side, pale and shaking, and remained silent. The officer went on: 'No one will ever know, you will go back home quietly and the secret will disappear with you. If you refuse that means immediate death. The choice is yours.' They remained motionless and silent.

Keeping calm, the Prussian went on, pointing to the river. 'Think, in five minutes' time you will be at the bottom of that river. In five minutes' time! You both have families, don't you?'

Mont Valerien was still booming.

The two fishermen remained standing in silence. The German gave orders in his own tongue. Then he moved his chair away from the prisoners and twelve men positioned themselves twenty paces away, rifles at the ready.

'I give you one minute, not a second more.'

Suddenly he got up, came towards the Frenchmen, grabbed Morissot's arm and taking him aside, whispered: 'Quick – the password. Your friend will not know, it will look as if I relented.'

Morissot did not answer.

The Prussian then took Mr Sauvage aside and asked him the same question. Mr Sauvage did not answer.

Once again they stood side by side.

The officer gave orders. The soldiers raised their guns.

At that moment Morissot happened to catch sight of the net full of fish left lying on the grass a few feet away.

A ray of sunshine made the still wriggling fish glisten and he suddenly felt weak. In spite of his efforts, tears welled in his eyes.

'Farewell, Mr Sauvage,' he faltered.

'Farewell, Mr Morissot,' answered Mr Sauvage.

They shook hands, trembling uncontrollably from head to foot.

'Fire!' shouted the officer.

The twelve shots sounded as one.

Mr Sauvage fell straight on his face. Mr Morissot, who was taller, swayed, pivoted and fell sideways across his friend's body, face up, with blood welling up from the hole in his chest.

The German gave further orders. His men scattered, then came back with ropes and stones which they tied to the feet of the two corpses, then they carried them to the river bank.

Mont Valerien continued to rumble, topped now by a mountain of smoke.

Four soldiers took hold of Morissot and Mr Sauvage by their arms and legs, swung them back then threw them as far as they could. The bodies curved in the air, hit the water feet first and sank rapidly, dragged down by the stones.

A splash, a few ripples and the water resumed its former calm as tiny waves reached the banks.

Calm and collected, the officer murmured: 'The fish will get even now.'

Then he walked back to the house.

Suddenly he saw in the grass the net full of fish. He picked it up, examined it, smiled and shouted: 'Wilhelm!'

A soldier in a white apron came running. The Prussian, throwing him the two friends' fish, ordered: 'Fry me these little things right away while they are still alive. They will be delicious.'

Then he went back to smoking his pipe.

Guy de Maupassant, *Two Friends, 1908.*

Fish Tales

The Roach Fisherman of the Fens

J.W. Martin – 'The Trent Otter' – was to coarse fishing what Skues and Halford were to fly fishing. He wrote beautifully about the streams and rivers of his native Midlands and the characters he met during a lifetime's devotion to fishing. Here he brings to life again a long dead brother of the angle.

Ship ahoy! ahoy! ahoy! rang out in hoarse but stentorian tones, waking the echoes in every direction and putting up a covey of partridges, which rose with one of those rattling whirrs that are so wont to startle unwary pedestrians. I gave an answering shout, and a little later a strange figure hove in sight which, a minute after, stood by my side. He was a man past the prime of life, but tall and erect as a pine, with a restless look about his keen grey eyes, which ever and anon kept sweeping the landscape in every direction, as though he were expecting a visitor from every point of the compass.

He must have been a splendid specimen of manhood in his younger days – over six feet high at sixty-five years of age, and as tough as his native pollards. Seaman and boatswain for many years in the navy, but now retired and enjoying a well-earned pension; his wooden leg peeped from under the bottom of his trousers, and as this limb reached higher than his knee and was not jointed, it gave a peculiar rolling gait to his walk. I looked upon that ancient mariner and fisherman with a veneration something akin to awe, for was he not the champion roach and tench angler of the fens in his day? and could he not spin the strangest and most awe-inspiring yarns of his adventures in many a strange land, by flood, frost, and field?

Nothing pleased him better than to have one or two of us in his cottage on a winter's evening, and bring out in vivid colours the story of his younger days, when hardships and press-gangs were everyday experiences; for he was a lonely man, with neither wife nor child. He was a devoted fisherman and a very successful one, and on this particular occasion we had been out for a couple of days, and had parted two hours previously, agreeing to meet at the spot where I was startled by his vigorous hail.

The little cottage in which he lived had been bought by him some years previously; it was only one storey high, with a couple of rooms and a back kitchen.

Standing a little back from the main road, in a small, well-kept garden, with a mass of woodbine trailing and climbing up the sides, over the top of the rustic porch, and far up the thatched roof, it looked a lovely little place, with such an air of peaceful quiet about it that an artist in search of a subject to illustrate 'Peace' would have grounded his easel and sketched it on the spot.

Inside, how strangely like the cabin of a ship it looked! A full-rigged model of a man-of-war of his day stood on a tall locker; two or three prints of Nelson's naval engagements and a curious old chart or map hung on the walls. The copper stove that stood under the mantelpiece was burnished to exceeding brightness, while here and there, on cunningly arranged shelves, was a large collection of marine shells of wonderful shape, size, and colour. In the other room a hammock swung in its net, and was fastened to the beam in the centre of the room by two huge iron hooks. Chairs there were none, but marvellously comfortable substitutes had been made on the lids of various lockers.

A well-known figure was the old man round that countryside, and occasionally anglers came from Spalding and elsewhere to enjoy a day's fishing with him during the season. But fish were plentiful and anglers scarce in those days, the majority of people holding anglers in great disdain, looking on them as a species of mild lunatic. Living memory goes back to the time when I could not see two anglers at once on all those miles of splendid fishing that stretched far and wide in every direction, and swarmed with fish of various kinds. In nearly the very heart of the fens of Lincolnshire, a few miles from the market town of Spalding, the old man's cottage stood, close to one of those canals that intersected that county nearly everywhere, and in those days literally swarmed with roach, tench, bream, perch, and pike. Good fishing could be had then anywhere, from Podehole engine across to Deeping; back again to Donington Bridge on the Fortyfoot, or from Podehole to Spalding, then across to Pinchbeck West; all down Vennatt's Drain, and right across to the river Welland – to say nothing of the districts nearer Holbeach; Peterborough, Peakirk, and away to Boston and Wisbeach; scores and scores of miles of excellent fishing. Since leaving that fenland district I have kept in touch with its fishing, getting odd notes and newspaper cuttings from a Spalding friend. One of these cuttings recorded the capture of six tench from Vennatt's Drain that went nearly twenty pounds; and another of twenty-four pounds of good-class roach, and forty-five pounds of bream; while later on in the season I found recorded a bag of eighteen perch that weighed twenty pounds, and half a dozen good jack at a single outing, that averaged five pounds per fish. In fact, on carefully going over these notes, I find that the whole district has not lost its charm, but to-day its old character is maintained, and frequent good takes are obtained in every direction.

Angling clubs and preservation societies were things I never heard about in my early fishing days; and one or two poachers occasionally roamed the district, but I think their depredations did not amount to much. Since those days the societies have taken over long stretches of water in every direction, nearly every town and large village on the banks having some local association, whose object is to preserve the fishing; permission to fish can be obtained on payment of a small daily or weekly sum in very many cases. One thing is in its favour – the district seems to be out of the beaten track; but still, holiday anglers might do worse than explore the locality. Suppose they made Spalding their objective; there is a good society there, with miles of water, and daily tickets at a small charge; and the railway runs in various directions from there, giving our wandering angler a wide field to choose from.

But I must return to my wooden-legged friend. This angler very seldom fished for anything except roach and tench, using a white paste of his own composition principally, varied occasionally with a few red worms or a handful of stewed wheat. The old man prided himself on that paste – he kept the secret of it to himself. I remember he used to chew up in his mouth a bit of white bread (it was generally brown or barley bread we got in those early days but the old man made his paste from white bread, working it up in a clean rag). He never used water, always wetting the bread by chewing in the mouth; then he would put a few drops of something in it from two very small bottles that he always carried with him, finally dabbing the paste into a pinch or two of flour, until he could work it into the required consistency. I have seen him go out and catch sixty roach in two hours with that paste; but then, on the other hand, I have also seen him catch a similar lot of roach in the same length of time on stewed wheat a little earlier in the season.

A rod with brass ferrules, and jointed, was a luxury not dreamed about at that time; we had to make our own.

Fish Tales

These were generally all in one piece, and about twelve feet long, the bottom part, nearest the hand grip, being a pine broom-handle planed and tapered; then a straight bit of hazel, some five or six feet, tapering from three-quarters of an inch in diameter to about three-eighths; and finally there were two feet of an old whalebone umbrella-rib as a springy tip. These joints were all spliced, glued, and whipped with fine cord; and I can remember, as if it was only yesterday, how proud the old man was of that rod. Reels and running lines were unknown – a yard or two of fine cord looped over a button at the tip end sufficed for him; his tackle, like the rod, was home-made. Good horsehair could very easily be procured in those days, and his nine or ten feet of horsehair line was such as I never saw anywhere else in all my wanderings.

The first three or four feet were composed of six hairs plaited carefully and smoothly together, the next of three hairs; then came a long length of two hairs twisted, and finally about two feet of the strongest and longest single white hair he could find, the joinings being spliced and whipped most carefully; and the hook at the end was an oldfashioned Kirby sneck bend. I remember that day he had just finished one of these lines, and lifted a two-pound weight with it; it was easily up to killing a three- or four-pound tench. Farm-horses in those days were different from what we see now; now they are all flesh and no hair to speak of; then they were raw-boned, with tails nearly reaching the ground.

A night or two before the incident recorded in the opening sentence of this chapter I had gone down to the old man's cottage, and found him busily engaged getting ready for our fishing trip, that was going to last a couple of days this time. Between Podehole and Gunn's Bridge, on the South Fortyfoot, was the place selected, where the roach were fairly plentiful and ran up to a good size; it was a very favourite spot of his, some little distance from the cottage in which he lived. Hook baits were all ready, and creature comforts in the old basket not forgotten. The old man's ground-bait varied very little from the one I use today; the lessons taught me then will never be eradicated – bread, bran, and a handful of meal, the whole flavoured with a penny packet of Thorley's pig food, which was all the rage in the Lincolnshire fens at that time; the whole being mixed together in stiffish balls.

Next morning we were up early, the sun just rising as we started for our one hour's tramp. Arriving, we commenced operations by quietly dropping half-a-dozen small balls of ground-bait, a little bigger than walnuts, in a beautiful place just over a long fringe of weeds. The water hardly anywhere is more than four or five feet deep, with no stream worth the name, a small goosequill carrying about three shots being ample to fish it. Sitting down on his basket, with the wooden leg sticking out in front like the barrel of a duck gun, he put on a kernel of wheat, and within five minutes a half-pound roach was kicking and gasping on the grass.

This was followed by another, and still another, so that within the half-hour eight or ten good fish were duly bagged. This was decidedly good business, setting my fingers on the itch; so the old man had no peace until he had cut me a suitable willow and fitted it up with a float and spare line. But, alas! my early efforts were not crowned with the success my enthusiasm deserved, for my share of the day's spoil did not assist the weight of the total bag by more than four or five pounds; but they were my first, or nearly so, and are to me a sacred memory that will never fade.

But the tutor was good and long-suffering and the pupil was willing, so improvement was rapid, and the day came, before very many seasons were over, when he had to put in all he knew to much overtop my catches. The fun went on that day more or less rapidly until the lengthening shadows warned us that it was time to suspend operations for that day and make preparations for the next. Counting up the spoil, we found nearly a hundred roach that would go a little more than three to the pound, and a brace of very fair tench. We were wondering what we should do with our fish; but on arriving at the little roadside inn where we were going to stay the night we found a fishmonger and his cart from Spalding there.

The man seemed glad to have them, giving us two or three shillings for the whole lot. Next morning we were again up early, and tramped along the bank to another favourite place, about two miles nearer home. This swim was just at the mouth of a small drain that ran from the higher lands, and had a most decided current down it. It was rather deeper just there than the usual thing in that canal, and was the old man's particular favourite. We did not get quite so many fish that day as we did on the previous day, but the majority of the roach were larger, and the basket was topped with five good tench, one of which I am certain went over three pounds, so what we lacked in numbers was made up in gross weight. Stewed wheat and white paste seemed to be about equally divided as bait there, the roach and tench taking both at times freely, particularly during the summer and early autumn.

This locality, as I said a page or two back, seems to me to be out of the beaten track, right away from the fashionable angling world and resorts; the angler who fished it would have to rough it I dare say, but in all likelihood the fishing would compensate. The South Fortyfoot that links up the country farmers between Podehole and Boston has many advantages to offer the wandering angler. I remember once a pike being captured on a dead gorge tackle not far from Donington Bridge, that reached over twenty pounds; and an annual visitor who stayed in a farmhouse opposite the lane end that leads to Donington Northorp captured many eels on night-lines that reached as heavy a weight as eight and nine pounds. I should say the roach fishing is still its chief charm, that visitor just named telling me that sometimes sport is so good that it gets monotonous. There was a little waterside public-house close to Donington Bridge, which may still exist and be very useful to intending visitors. This house, I fancy, is about half-way between Podehole and Boston, and on either hand for miles stretches a water that ought to please anybody. It was not far from there that I landed my first roach; I can see the place in my mind's eye now, close to an old black water-mill, hard by Ridley's Farm.

The country, taking it on the whole, is rather flat and uninteresting. The canal is not very wide nor yet deep, four joints of a roach pole or an eleven-foot Nottingham rod being sufficient anywhere. I fancy since I left that way the water is preserved by some association other than the Spalding one, but I think the charge is only a shilling for the whole season. The old wooden-legged pensioner and I roamed for miles along those banks one time or other, and I owe him a debt of gratitude that I never repaid. He instilled into my young life that love of fish, fishing, and nature that sticks to me even now when the locks on my brow have turned grey.

I could not help giving this chapter the pride of place in this book, as some little acknowledgment of what I owe to him and his humane teachings and example. Circumstances over which I had no control caused me to drift away from the place, and it was years after when I next set foot upon the familiar ground. Alas! the old cottage was remodelled, and had passed into a stranger's hands, who knew not the wizard of the rod who once owned it. The porch, with its trailing woodbine, was a thing of the past; the grass was growing green over the place where they had laid him; and I turned away with a lump in my throat and a whispered prayer that the earth might lightly lie on one of the best who ever walked its surface.

J.W. Martin ('The Trent Otter'), *My Fishing Days and Fishing Ways*, 1906.

Dace Fishing at Isleworth

The simplicity and unambitiousness of the fishing described so beautifully in the next extract makes it my own favourite piece of angling writing. Anyone who knows the place here described will understand how much we have lost as London has expanded and swallowed up the fields and woods of Surrey.

The angler might travel very much farther and fare very much worse. That is my thought every time I visit Isleworth fly-rod in hand, and it is strange if

Fish Tales

September or October does not find me there at least once in each year. I have made the expedition pretty often now, but the charm of it never fails; it is like nothing that I know in the way of fishing near London. Nowhere else can one feel that one is literally cheating Fate out of a few happy hours. When one goes farther afield, to the Colne, perhaps, at West Drayton, Uxbridge, or Rickmansworth, there is the sense of an undertaking about it; one is earning the right to enjoyment by dint of railway travelling, by having made 'arrangements', by being burdened with a landing-net and possibly lobworms – one is definitely out for the day. But Isleworth is a simple, unpremeditated sort of matter. At luncheon-time one has a sudden conviction that too much work is telling on one's health, and that an afternoon off is the right medicine. A glance at the paper tells one that the tide was high at London Bridge at half-past nine; a simple calculation proves that, since it is an hour later at Richmond, the Isleworth shallows will begin to be fishable at about two.

A light ten-foot rod, a reel, fly-box, and basket take no long time to collect; the rubber knee-boots stand ready in their corner. One is equipped and away almost as soon as the idea has been formed.

It matters little that the train stops at all stations, and that the carriages are primitive almost to archaism. *En route* for Richmond these things are just and proper. One likes to see people getting in and out full of business. Even if one does not quite understand why anyone living in Gunnersbury should apparently be in such a hurry, so impatient to get to Kew Gardens and urgent affairs, this does not mar the sense of personal emancipation; rather it enhances it by contrast.

One could get out at Kew Gardens oneself, by the way, walk down to the towpath, and fish up to Isleworth, and I have done this once or twice. But I prefer on the whole to go on to Richmond now and walk downstream. Richmond has made efforts of late to get into line with the times, but mercifully its fascination will not easily be destroyed. Modernity mellows there by the side of age better than in almost any place I know. As a matter of fact, one sees little of the town, for almost opposite the station yard is a gate leading to the old deer park. It is about ten minutes' walk across the park to the towpath, which one strikes just above the lock, and yet ten minutes more to the church ferry at the bottom of Isleworth eyot. Above the lock there are always anglers, but I have never yet seen one of them actually catch anything at the time of my passing. From below it one can see the weir, the only one on the Thames which has not moved in me the desire of trout. At high water, however, it looks as if it ought to hold one or two, and there certainly are trout in the reach, though systematic trout-fishing does not seem to go on there. I remember once seeing a big trout feed at the head of the eyot, but whether he is still in existence I know not. Almost any day at low water, however, below the eyot there are alarms and excursions to be seen among the dace, which argue fish of prey of considerable size, trout probably. Occasionally, too, a trout is caught by a dace-fisher, but it is usually a small one.

Arrived at the ferry, it is well to cross over and fish on the other side, and the knowledgeable make their way down for a third of a mile or perhaps rather more to the point where the river is shallowest, just above a slight but recognizable bend in the stream. Here, they say, are the biggest dace, the six-ounce fish, which, when caught, are to be found at the top in each man's basket, like half-pound trout in Devonshire. But I should say that there is a fair sprinkling of these big dace all the way down, the difficulty being to catch them. Some men hold by big flies, coachmen, black gnats, yellow duns, etc., on No. 1 or even No. 2 hooks being considered about right, and more than once I have been tempted to the same opinion. Lately, however, the big fly has not served me well. On my last visit nothing but a black spider on a tiny hook would do any good. That afternoon also upset another theory, or, rather, taught me something new. My belief had been that you could catch the Isleworth dace in two ways – one with the dry or semi-dry fly, in which case the fish usually took it on the drop or half volley, as some authority puts it, or wet and drawn along more or less rapidly under water. For a while they confirmed me in this belief, and I caught several with the dry fly, while I missed a good many in the other way.

Then they ceased to come up to it at all, either wet or dry, until I accidentally got a rise in recovering the fly as it floated. This led to experiments, and I found that, by letting the fly fall dry and then dragging it for a few inches along the surface, I got plenty of rises, and pretty bold ones too. The fish came at it before it had gone six inches or not at all, and for an hour I had quite a brisk bit of sport, so much so that on reaching the ferry I did not hesitate to estimate the number of fish kept as three dozen. I was really surprised, on counting tails afterwards, to find that there were only a dozen and a half. It had seemed to me that for a time I was catching them as fast as I could. Three dozen would be a very fair basket for a good day, though takes of eight or ten dozen are made once in a way. Six inches is the size limit, and the majority of fish caught are about seven. If your three dozen average three ounces apiece, you have done very well indeed, and if you have three or four six-ounce fish you may be proud. There are plenty of these big ones in the water, but they are difficult to tempt.

It is worth while catching a dish of these little dace, if only for the pleasure of looking at them afterwards. They make a brave silvery show when laid side by side, and though individually at time of capture they have not the looks of brook trout, collectively in the evening they have the advantage. Brook trout lose their gold, but dace preserve their silver. One good angler informed me (rather apologetically), that he proposed to have his catch to breakfast. No apology was needed, for, bones admitted and extracted, dace are good meat – as good as many trout.

But dace are not the whole of Isleworth fishing. There is the daily wonder of the great river shrinking away so that a man may go dry-foot (or practically so) along its gravel bed, to see only a clear, shallow stream where a few hours back was a deep, turbid flood; there is the awful pleasure of imagining what would happen if one were caught suddenly by the turn of the tide, for one is so low down in the world that it seems wellnigh impossible to climb up that steep bank through the mud to the grounds of Zion House; there is the wonderful solitude almost within sound of London – a small human figure or so up at the ferry, perhaps, and about the brown-sailed barges at the distant quay, but for the rest no sign of life except a gull or two wheeling round, some rooks exploring the naked river-bed, and the dace dimpling the surface of the quiet stream.

Then, when the tide has turned (and may you be not too far from the ferry when that happens!), there is a late tea at the London Apprentice, the quaint old inn near the church. The view from its billiard-room window up stream and down is alone worth the journey. After it there is the return in the ferry-boat, with a long backward look at the riverside street and the old church beneath their canopy of crimson sky; the meditative walk back along the towpath under the great trees, almost each one sheltering its couple of shy lovers who are making believe that the world is as they would have it be; the crossing of the old green, with its circle of fair dwellings; and lastly, the extraordinary blaze of light as one gets to the corner of the green and looks up towards the town. This is a fitting end to a day of impressions that one does not easily forget.

H.T. Sheringham, *An Open Creel*, 1910.

A Day of Tribulation

It is mercifully ordained that one's keenest memories are in general of things pleasant. The angler in reminiscent mood loves to dwell on big baskets, soft western breezes, and the other outstanding features of a roseate past. The things he has suffered in the pursuit of his recreation have left but little impression behind, and in retrospect seem but little clouds on the mental horizon. This is as it should be, for if the remembrance of pains were as vivid as the remembrance of pleasures, a man would seriously begin to wonder whether it was worth while. Yet, in spite of this beneficent ordinance of fate, there must be always days in one's angling history that one still regards with horror and indignation – days which no amount of subsequent joy has availed to obliterate.

It has always seemed to me that an undue number of them falls to my share, but this may not be a real philosophical discovery, for I have heard other men complain, apparently with some reason. The worst days of all I group roughly together; they represent the limited number of occasions on which I have sworn a solemn oath to give up fishing for ever. In addition to their own inherent vileness they must, therefore, also bear the responsibility of several solemn oaths having been broken, though this last is not a charge that I would wish to press too seriously. It would have been a pity if an oath made in haste of an evening had seemed more than an expression of impatience at breakfast-time on the morrow. Only once do I remember really giving up fishing in consequence

Completely stumped. A classic fishing illustration from about 1890

of a malign day, and in agreement with a vow made in the darkness of despair. The events that led up to the proceeding were these:

I was staying in the West Country for a fortnight's trout-fishing at the end of April. Several days had passed like some pleasant dream.

The weather had been perfect, and the trout of the country fairly amenable, so that every evening I was able to display a half-pounder or so, besides the ordinary tale of takeable fish – they ran about five to the pound, and one of half a pound was an achievement. Therefore, lulled into a kind of false security, I was ill-prepared for the day when adversity came rushing against me on the wings of a northerly gale.

I started by trudging four miles in wading-stockings and brogues, a tedious form of exercise. But the day before, while taking a Sunday stroll, I had seen a perfectly monstrous trout, four pounds if an ounce, and he had decided my movements for the Monday. However, when the four miles were covered, I found that the wind was tearing straight down the valley, and making it quite impossible to get a fly at him. He had to be approached from below, for over-hanging trees almost met above his haunt, and no wet-fly line could be cut into the teeth of the wind. I therefore did not attempt to cover him but waited until there should come a lull, and, in the meantime, began to fish downstream with three flies.

I never had a great deal of skill in downstream fishing, and I was not sur-prised when almost at once a good trout robbed me of the second dropper. Nor was I surprised when, on searching for the damping-box, in which I had put some spare flies to soften the gut, I found that it had been left behind. Accidents of this kind will happen, so I shrugged my shoulders, took out my fly-book, and began to disentangle half a dozen Greenwell's glories, which had got themselves into hopeless confusion. After a good deal of patient work I extricated one and put the gut into my mouth. Then the other five blew away and vanished utterly. As they represented my remaining stock of this valuable fly, I spent half an hour in looking for them. Then I shrugged my shoulders once more, fastened on the dropper, and returned to the fishing. In less than a minute my last Greenwell was gone in another fish. The fly-book was open once more, and a blue upright was taken out, while three red palmers were blown out, never to be seen again – by me, at all events. Looking for them, however, occupied a certain amount of time, and it was fully twenty minutes before I got to fishing again.

So far I had been content to let my line float out with the wind and settle on the water where it would; but now I desired to reach an eddy behind a big stone close to the opposite bank. To this end I attempted a cast across the wind, and failed utterly. A collar of three flies wrapped round one is an awkward thing to deal with, especially if, as in my case, the tail-fly is fixed in a wading-sock, the first dropper in the landing-net, and the second in the small of one's back.

It took me some time to rearrange matters, to replace the second dropper, which broke when I was taking off my coat, and to hunt for the four red spinners which I had the misfortune to lose when I opened my fly-book. But at last I got to work again, and began to realize that, in spite of the gale, the fish were rising in a remarkable manner. Almost every time the flies touched the water I could feel a pluck, but never a fish hooked himself or allowed me to hook him, until at last a big fellow took the tail-fly with a plunge.

There may be men who, during a gale, can control a three-quarter pound trout at the end of a long line downstream in rough water on gossamer gut, but I am not one of them, and very soon I was searching for the six hare's ears that had been blown out of my book while I was selecting a new tail-fly.

I did not find them, and there is no need for me to describe the search. It resembled the searches that had preceded it and those that came after. Never in my life have I lost so many flies in one morning, and I believe that I have never risen and lost a greater number of fish. They seemed madly on the feed, and had it been only possible to fish upstream, I am certain I should have made a big basket. As it was I pricked trout, played them, lost flies in them, and did everything but land them. Finally I left a whole cast in a bush over deep water, and retired from the unequal contest. I judged it well to give myself time to get calm, if that were possible, so I withdrew to the foot of the moorland hill, sat down with my back to the river, and endeavoured to think of Job. It seemed to me that I could have comforted him a little by contrasting his case with mine, though I did not see where any comfort was to come from for me. But by meditating on one's wrongs I suppose one gets comforted automatically, and presently I plucked up enough spirit to eat my sandwiches, and they did me good.

The discovery that I had left my flask behind with the damping-box seemed but a slight thing in comparison with the tremendous evils of the morning, and I drank a draught of pure water from a rill trickling through the moss resignedly.

After this I began to realize that the wind had dropped a little, and at once thought of my fourpounder. If only he could be caught the rest did not matter. A new cast was selected and soaked in the rill, and to it I attached a good big March brown. Then I returned to the river, and made my way upstream to the monster's haunt. He lay at the head of a long still pool, and from watching him the day before I had gathered that he moved up into the ripple to feed, and that he had a certain beat. I intended, therefore, to fish carefully up this beat,

The angler's enemy – an irate bull. From Joseph Crawhall's Victorian work *The Completest Angling Book that Ever was Writ*

trusting to find him somewhere along it. The wind was now considerably abated, and by wading along one side under the bushes, and casting across and upstream, it was possible to cover the necessary expanse of water. This I proceeded to do, and as this is a tale of woe there is no need to dwell on details. The fish, or a fish of great size, at any rate, was just where I expected, took the fly with a rush, ran out twenty yards of line, leaped twice, ejected the fly, and was gone in about half a minute, leaving me to my thoughts of Job and his exaggerated griefs.

After this I wandered upstream for a long way without troubling to fish until the crowning misfortune of the day fell upon me. For some distance the river had run through open moorland, but now I came to a field and surmounted a stile. Halfway across I became aware of approaching thunder, and, looking round, perceived that a herd of cattle was stampeding in my direction, apparently of set purpose.

To avoid unprofitable argument, I stepped hurriedly down the steep bank into the river, which was just not deep enough to overtop my waders. The cattle reached the bank above, and watched me with indignation as I began to make my way across. Then, as though by concerted arrangement, a fresh enemy appeared on the other side – a big, evil-looking black dog, which had the air of one accustomed to protect homesteads. It stood and waited for me in grim silence. Then it was that I took the solemn oath to give up fishing, not only for that day, but for all time, if only I should win safely out of my parlous situation. I have no doubt that there was nothing to fear from either dog or cattle, but my nerves were upset by calamity.

The rest is a tale of splashing downstream until I got back to the moor below the cattle and away from the dog. Incidentally I broke the top of my rod and filled my waders, and had to walk home in dire discomfort and in heavy rain. As to the solemn oath, it was kept for a whole day. The day after, however, was the perfection of fishing weather, and the river had fined down nicely.

H.T. Sheringham, *An Open Creel*, 1910.

In Praise of Chub

Much water has eddied under the bridges, foamed over the weirs, and lost itself in the Severn sea since first I came under the spell. But the water must flow longer and stronger yet to wash away recollection of that solemn time. It was high summer on Shakespeare's stream, and afternoon – poetically, it was always afternoon in a lotus-land where white canvas alone shut out the stars of night, but on this occasion prosaically also, for luncheon was over and done with – when from afar I first espied loggerhead basking at ease just outside the spreading willow. No novice was I at the sport of angling, but had taken as many brave fish as most boys of my years, with now and again a pounder among them, while I boasted acquaintance with a veteran angler who had that summer slain a cheven of full two pounds. But here was something which passed my experience – a chub of unparalleled magnitude in a land where the community spoke with respect of pounders. He had length, breadth, and dignity; he lay at the surface an imposing bulk, and for a while I stood spellbound.

Then the natural boy asserted itself, and sought a plan of campaign. Now you must know that cheven is, in some respects, the wisest of fishes, and when he suns himself at the top he is impatient of intruders. But a glimpse of Piscator or of the angle-rod outlined against the sky, and he is gone, sunk quietly out of sight and reach. Strategy, therefore, demands that Piscator should grovel, trailing the angle-rod behind, into some concealed position, whence the fly may be artfully despatched.

Like the earth-worm, I wriggled down the grassy slope to the little bush which offered the only bit of cover on the bank, and, peeping round it, found, to my relief, that loggerhead was still in view. But he was a long way off –

Leaping chub, by A. Rowland Knight

twenty yards at least – and even had I been able to cast so far with the little nine-foot rod – 'suitable to youths' – and the light line, there was the rising ground behind to frustrate me. There was nothing for it but to wait in the hope that the fish might come a little nearer. So I waited, and I will not say that a prayer was not breathed to Poseidon that he should send loggerhead towards my bank. A long time I waited – maybe half an hour or more – and the fish never moved more than an inch or two, but at long last he seemed to wake up. Some trifle of a fly attracted his attention, and I saw capacious jaws open and shut, and afterwards he seemed anxious for more, for he began to cruise slowly about. Then by slow degrees the circles of his course widened, until finally he was within about twelve yards of my bank. Now, I judged, was the time, and with a mighty effort and heart in mouth I switched out the fly at the end of my line (an artificial bluebottle, I remember) as far as I could.

It fell quite a yard short, but that mattered little. Round he came sharply to see what had happened, steadily he swam up to the bluebottle, boldly he opened his mouth, and then I drank indeed the delight of battle. Three pounds he weighed all but an ounce, which doesn't matter, and for quite a time I fondly preserved his skin, adequately peppered and salted, as I thought, but in the end elders and betters intervened with forcible remarks about nuisances. So I was left with his memory only, of which nobody could rob me. From that day I have revered the chub, and so often as the hot summer days come round (there are not so many of them as there were when Plancus was Consul), so often do I bethink me of the sunlit waters, the cool willow shades, the fresh scent of waterweeds from the weir, the hum of bees, and, above all, the dark forms lying on the surface ready for the fly.

Some there are who will give you hard words concerning the chub, having, maybe, hooked him on Wye just in the V of the currents where they fondly expected a salmon, having perchance frayed the gossamer trout-cast all to tatters in keeping his brute strength out of the roots, and having disturbed twenty good yards of water to boot. But these unfortunates (I grant them the title) have encountered cheven out of his proper sphere, and their sympathies are warped thereby. Heed them not, but seek him in his rightful rivers, slow-flowing, rush-lined, lily-crowned, girt with willows and rich pastures; take with you your stoutest single-handed fly rod, strong gut, and big palmer flies, or coachman, alder, zulu – it matters little so the mouthful be big and so it have a small cunning tail of white kid; go warily along the bank with eye alert for a dark form under yon clay bank, in that little round hole among the lilies, beneath that tree, above that old log – anywhere, in fact, where a worthy fish may combine ease with dignity and, possibly, nutriment. Having found him, pitch your fly at him with as much tumult as you please; if he does not see you or the rod, two to one he will rise. If he does see you he is gone, and herein lies most of the fascination of it. A stiff neck and a proud stomach are of no use to the chub-fisher, who must stoop if he wishes to conquer. With good luck you should catch a three-pounder, among others, with very good luck a four-pounder. Those who are what Horace Walpole, I believe, called serendipitous catch a five-pounder now and again. The favoured of the gods get a six-pounder once in their lives. And one or two anglers, for whose benefit the whole cosmic scheme has evidently been arranged, have killed a seven-pounder. But this last prodigy does not, I fancy, reward fly-fishing, though I once – but the memory is too bitter to be evoked. Cheese paste is the thing for seven-pounders if you know of any such, and you can put a piece on the hook of your fly if you like. But you cannot throw it very far, the fishing is difficult, and I much doubt whether they are seven-pounders. Your basking chub is so imposing that one's estimate of his ounces is insensibly coloured by awe. I have ever been curious to know how big was the chub which Walton and his pupil gave to Maudlin the milkmaid.

The only indication vouchsafed to us is that it was 'just such another' as the first one, with a white spot on its tail, and that was the biggest of twenty – all lying together in one hole. From this slender store of evidence I deduce it to have been two and a half pounds, because that is commonly the doyen in so numerous a shoal.

The monsters do not often crowd so close as a score together. Four and five pounders are, I think, to be observed four or five in company, not more. How it may be with seven-pounders I know not; likely they swim in pairs, a pair to a mile of river, and that the best mile. I do not know of a pair, but I know of one which a good friend of mine captured in a recent year. It weighed seven pounds and a quarter, and constituted the gravest angling tragedy which has come under my notice in a decade, for the month was May, and my friend is a very

'I have ever been curious to know how big the chub was
which Walton . . . gave to Maudlin'

honest man. So the monster was gently returned, and some day will no doubt
be the father of all the chub.

Loggerhead is a noble, pleasant fish, of thoughtful habit, and he gives
right good sport to those who seek him with discretion, but he has, they say,
his weak points. On the table – yet is this an angler's matter? All that con-
cerns Piscator in the treatise of culinary wisdom is surely the first injunc-
tion, 'First catch him.' Caught, I have never found him otherwise than welcome to the descendants of sweet-throated Maudlin. It needs to inquire no
further.

The finest sport I have ever had with chub was on a kind of April day set by
accident in the middle of August. The wind blew with a certain amount of
vehemence from the south-west; it was none too warm, and the lights and
shadows caused by alternation of sunshine and cloud were far more suggestive
of spring than of summer. It would have been an excellent day for trout, but it
hardly promised great sport with chub. Still, the fortnight of August that had

A coarse fishing scene – a weir on the Sussex Ouse near Barcombe Mills, by Bernard Venables

preceded this April day had provided no chub weather worth mentioning. What sun there had been was of pale and watery complexion, with great cloud-banks hovering near, ready to obscure him if he showed any sign of cheerfulness at all. The wind also had been cold and violent, and fly-fishing had been a mockery.

The April day, therefore, was at least an improvement, and the split-cane rod was put together with more cheerfulness of spirit. It would not be a case of stalking fish scientifically, for they would hardly be on the surface; but there was a chance that a big fly thrown into likely spots might bring up a brace or two of decent chub, and give the angler something to show for his pains. In these incredulous days it is sadly necessary to have something to show, and I was growing a little tired of explaining to the lay mind that success cannot be commanded when the weather is unpropitious.

Besides, it is thankless work giving explanations that are obviously misunderstood.

Accordingly I was resolute to catch something when I reached the bridge that spanned the Thames – here a mere infant river – with two small arches.

Under the bridge the stream rippled in a manner provokingly suggestive of trout; but though there is much water that might well hold a head of fario in the topmost reaches of the river, the head of fario is conspicuously wanting. A trout has occasionally been taken as high as this, but Lechlade, a good deal lower down, is the first point where the fish becomes a calculable possibility. Beyond regretting this fact, therefore, I took no thought of trout, but looked upstream for a sign of rising chub.

Above the sharp water at the bridge is a long, quiet pool, and in its lower corner, on the left bank, is a clump of bushes growing right down into the water, and forming a splendid harbour. A rise was soon seen just below the bushes, and then another, and presently it became evident that the fish were moving.

Leaving the bridge, I got into the meadow opposite, from which it was possible to attain a small strip of shingle below, and within casting distance of the bushes. Before the edge was approached, however, some twenty yards of line were pulled off the reel and anointed with deer's fat. Since the chub were rising, they might just as well be attacked with a dry fly. This is, perhaps, an unnecessary refinement for chub; and, indeed, it is not by any means always that they will take a floating fly properly, but when they do the sport is not to be despised.

Preparations complete, and a biggish coachman oiled and attached to a cast that tapered to the finest undrawn gut, the river was approached, and the attack begun. The strip of shingle was about fifteen yards from the last bush, and the distance was soon found. Then the fly dropped close to the submerged twigs. There was no delay on the part of the chub, for a heavy fish plunged at the coachman the instant it touched the water. So sudden was the response that the line was not released by the fingers holding it against the rod-butt, and a vigorous strike proved too much for the gut. Another plunge, and the chub was gone with the coachman. This was vexatious, for the loss of a fish that has been hooked generally frightens the shoal. The rule is not quite invariable, however, so another fly was put on and cast a little higher up, in the hope that the other chub might not have noticed the little contretemps. This seemed to be the case, for a rise followed immediately.

There was no mistake about the strike this time, and the reel screamed as the hook went home, continuing to scream as the fish dashed off. A chub's first rush is formidable, and with fine gut it is no good trying to stop it; but if the fish does not break, then it ought to be landed safely and speedily. Before long the fight was over, and a fish of one and a half pounds was in the net, tapped on the head, and thrown out into the meadow, where the creel had been left.

Then the fly was again thrown towards the bushes. Another fish took it immediately, and was landed in the same manner as the first, to which it might have been a twin brother. Then two smaller ones, of about one and a quarter pounds, each came to the net, and were returned. In a good chub river nothing under one and a half pounds is really worth keeping, unless local taste in the matter of fish-diet is very responsive; but big chub will sometimes find grateful recipients in the country, as will be seen. After the brace of small ones had been returned a two-pounder was landed, and after that several more fish of about one and a half pounds.

By the end of half an hour there must have been a dozen or more on the bank, and the sport showed no sign of slackening. Another two-pounder was just in the net when an exclamation was heard from the bridge. A cyclist had paused to look on, and was much impressed with the sight of somebody actually catching something. 'What a beauty!' he said, as the chub was thrown out into the meadow after the rest. This remark suggested that a heaven-sent opportunity was at hand. 'Would you care about some fish?' I asked guilelessly. The cyclist nodded with strange enthusiasm, and was warmly pressed to help himself. He clambered down over the wall with his mackintosh cape, into which he packed the fish with some grass. He was full of gratitude at being told to take them all, and departed, bearing some twenty pounds of chub at his saddle-bow, and leaving me to reflect that appreciation of true merit is hard to find, but when found, pleasant to contemplate.

After he had gone fishing was resumed. A fish plunged at the coachman, but would not take it. It was so obviously bigger than anything caught so far that it seemed worth while to change the fly, and several patterns were tried in vain. At last a wet fly, a big alder, with a wash-leather tail, was put on, and cast in with a plop just where the fish had risen. A wave came out from the bushes at once, the line tightened, and a gentle strike fastened the hook into something better worth catching. The fish showed plenty of fight, but after one rush under the twigs, from which a steady strain brought it out, there was no real danger, and before long a plump three-pounder was landed. He was deemed worthy of a place in the big creel, and was accordingly killed and put in. After this, sport with the wet fly was quite as brisk as it had been with the coachman, and the fish were bigger – nothing under two pounds, and the biggest weighing three and a half pounds.

To sum up, by the time the rise was over the twenty-two pound creel was full to the brim, and half a dozen chub beside had to be carried home on a withy twig. All these fish, weighing, with those given away, at least fifty pounds, had been caught without moving from the strip of shingle, and without fishing more than fifteen yards of water, which only shows how chub may be caught when they are really on the feed.

The last cast provoked a curious conclusion to a wonderful morning. A fish followed the fly just like a chub, took it, and was played to the net, when it proved to be a small pike of about two and a half pounds. It gave a last kick as the net was about to receive it, the frayed gut parted, and the fly which had caught so many fish vanished for ever.

H.T. Sheringham, *An Open Creel*, 1910.

Three children fishing from a river bank, by William Bromley

A Curious Madness

Here H.T. Sheringham describes, as well as anyone ever has, the child's delight in fishing.

Of all the unlikely places – and yet perhaps not so unlikely after all. For in this land of waters you might meet with sport almost anywhere, even out in the fields if you chose to angle at large when the floods come, as they are pretty sure to do somewhere between January and March.

In front of us is a river, to right and left of us is a canal. At the back of us is another river. Eastwards is a big lake, westwards a series of fish ponds. Everywhere are streams and ditches more or less filled with water and inhabited by fish.

Fish Tales

But Guy's fishery is the least of them all. Where the road rises to cross the railway there are two culverts, one on each side of the wooden steps at the end of the walk by which we get out of the garden. That on the left is quite considerable, carrying back to the river a tolerable stream maybe six feet wide and a foot deep. Doubtless there are good fishes in that stream, for the dace will work up early in the year and some probably stay there all the summer. If Guy had made this his preserve there would be no cause for surprise. But it is the other culvert which attracts him; a mere trifle of a pipe eighteen inches wide, with the water (in these days of drought) coming to a dead end a few feet below it. Just at the culvert's mouth is a yard of fishable water six inches deep.

'Fishing? *There?*' was the natural comment when the project was first mooted.

'Yes, there, certainly', was the reply, and so tempting was the description of the sport, so vivid the account of fishes seen, so real the three-inch dace, the minnow, and the two sticklebacks in the jam jar, that it was then and there decided to make a party of pleasure and to invite the catcher of chubs thereto, on condition that he provide tackle and do all that was necessary about worms. This angling is a curious madness. Why it comes over some and spares others it is hard to say, but it is probable that those who are spared have never sat with goggling eyes and baited breath watching a live fish in the clear water approach the suspended worm and poise in doubt before it. The yearning then is simply fearful, and if the fish, having doubted enough, turns away, the impulse to down and at it with a net is almost irresistible. The party of pleasure sits on the brick wall of the culvert and looks down with greedy eyes. In full view there are three minnows and five sticklebacks. A stickleback tweaks the First Angler's worm, but it will not come to serious grips with it. Serious grips with a stickleback means a slow laborious swallowing of half a worm. Then all the angler has to do is to lift the line steadily from the water and the stickleback comes with it. The fish is in the ridiculous position of having stuffed himself so full that he cannot part with his prey and he therefore has to hang on despite himself.

Today, however, no stickleback shows genuine interest.

'Guy, you're frightening them,' says the First Angler. Indeed Guy's lure *is* leaping up and down in the water in an agitated manner. Doubtless good Father Walton knew how difficult it is to keep the point of one's peastick quiet and steady when one is awfully anxious to catch a fish. Probably his Scholar did much the same sort of thing when he watched the chub with a white spot on its tail. If your fish won't come to the worm, make the worm pursue the fish – that is a very natural and pardonable theory, even if it does not succeed.

'There were *much* bigger ones,' says the First Angler, 'like that one we caught. And spotted ones too.' And Guy is persuaded to lay his peastick down so that the little red worm may lie temptingly on the bottom. Then, perhaps, from under the arch . . . 'Look, did you see *that*?' Yes, indeed, we all saw. It was like a giant among the minnows, but it went back under the arch at once. '*That* was a spotted one. Oh, and there's one of the others, two, three. Guy, *leave* your rod alone. Of *course* they won't take it if you jump it about. You've frightened them away again.'

Even as this complaint is made, there is a scurry under the arch, out dashes a fish, seizes the First Angler's worm, and in a moment is flying up into the middle air, its scales flashing in the sunlight as it goes. 'Let me see. May I put it in the bottle. What is it? Isn't it a nice fish? Is it as big as the one we got yesterday? Can I catch one too? Shall we put it in the tank?' Never did a three inch dace cause a greater volume of talk.

Guy has to discuss the affair from every aspect, and to pick the creature out of its jam jar three times before he feels that the incident is closed. Then we all go back to our fishing.

There is an interval of peace and quiet.

And then, 'Oh, I've got one.' Guy positively squeals with excitement. But, alas, he has been too precipitate. The stickleback has no more than got the end of the worm into its mouth and it falls back with a tiny splash. 'Oh, I want the net. *Please* let me catch it with the net. I *do* want to catch it.'

The shrimp net is there for emergencies, but not for mere revenge like this. 'No, you'd only disturb the water. You wait a bit, and you'll catch something better than the stickleback in a minute.'

'Shall I catch one like yours?' He is assured that he will if he displays the proper angler's patience. And so we dispose ourselves to wait again with our eyes earnestly on the mouth of the culvert.

It is a glorious day. The sun pours down upon us and the bricks on which we sit are warm to the hand. The air is full of the humming of insects and the chirp of grasshoppers in the long grass of the bank. A robin has hopped on to the stile to see what we are doing and to find out if there is anything to his advantage in it. Just beyond the hedge there is a steady munching, most comfortable of sounds. The great cart horses in the field have drawn up to the shade to continue their dinner. They are company for the lonely party of fishers, or they would be if needed.

But they are not needed, for see, where a whole troop of fishes comes out from the arch, several like the one in the bottle and three spotted ones. Now for it! These be tense moments as all the fishes swim about the two worms, now seeming to notice them, now apparently ignoring them. The minnows and sticklebacks have given way before their betters and are gone into the weeds below. The great ones have the pool all to themselves. But they do not bite, unhappily, and presently they are again vanished, and nothing done.

This is a bad business. We are annoyed. Who ever before saw so many fish and two worms and no bites? It is not to be borne. Let us – but no, the culvert goes right under the road, and the handle of the shrimp net is only four feet long. It would be useless to scoop, for the fishes would simply swim out of reach. Let us rather try another dodge. Now, see that fly on the brick. Advance a hand very cautiously behind him, now a quick dashing encirclement – so. Pinch him for pity's sake, and let us put him on the hook instead of the worm. Now let him down till he rests on the surface of the water, and wait. Here come all the fishes again, and at once there is a bold swirl, the fly has vanished, and behold another silvery inmate for the jam jar. It is great medicine, as we anglers say, this dibbling with a fly.

But it cannot always be administered. For the life of us we cannot catch another fly, and we have to rebait with a worm, a little wriggly pink one this time. It serves though. Hardly is it on the bottom when out comes the biggest of all the company of fishes and is gone with it under the arch. But not for long. The First Angler grasps the peastick with both hands, tightens lips, and pulls. And so there is another fish for the bottle, the greatest yet. 'Is that a gudgeon? What's a gudgeon? Is it bigger than a dace? It's all blue and silver. Can I have it in my hand?' Guy celebrates this great capture in his accustomed manner. Truly it is worth celebrating, for the gudgeon measures four inches, no less.

After this there is another spell of idleness. The fishes come out as before from time to time, but they seem uneasy in their minds. Perhaps they miss their late companions. Anyhow they take no notice of either of the worms. Fishing begins to seem a slow business. It feels as though it must be getting on for tea-time.

'It *can't* be tea-time,' protests Guy, 'till I've caught a fish. You *said* I would catch one.'

Here is an awkward situation. It is quite true. There *was* a prophecy. Of all the rash speeches – for if fishing teaches you nothing else it teaches you the unwisdom of being confident. Why, men spend whole weeks at it sometimes and catch nothing at all. There are men who have spent years trying to catch a Thames trout and are still waiting for one to bite. And Guy was promised that he should catch fish 'in a minute'. This is a bad business and faces grow long.

Then we are suddenly aroused to interest by strange events in the water. Away under the arch out of sight there is a commotion which results in waves coming out into the pool. And with them come all the fishes in a great hurry. Guy tries to make his worm hurry too, but is persuaded to put the peastick down again. The fishes go round the pool and vanish once more. 'There's something up in there', is the sage if not very illuminating comment.

All becomes quiet again, and minds are bent on the problem, how to satisfy Guy without a fish. It is clear that none of the company below is willing to oblige. They are all obviously completely out of humour.

And then, without any warning, there is a fresh excitement. Something incredibly large dashes out from the arch, grabs Guy's worm, and bolts back with it, pulling the point of the peastick down as it goes. There is great confusion. We all jump about, and cry aloud, clutch at the peastick, give advice, exclaim, pull, heave, and finally exult. For look what we have flouncing before us on the grass. It is a noble perch, with red fins, black stripes, and well armed back. It is seven inches long. It is much bigger than the gudgeon. It could *eat* the gudgeon, very nearly. It is almost worth cooking. And Guy has caught it. Didn't we *tell* him he would catch one in a minute? True, we never hoped for quite such a fish as this. It will hardly go into the bottle, except standing on its head. Never mind, there is plenty of room in the tank.

Now, we can go back to tea with complete satisfaction. We have done all that we set out to do. Aye and more also. For from this day forward Guy is sealed of the brotherhood of anglers. The madness that came upon him in his sixth year will be with him when he numbers three score and ten. This may be for good or for ill, but the thing is done now. 'I fish very well,' observes the angler complacently as he trots along homewards hugging the jam jar.

Fortunately this dangerous form of pride will not last. Some day he will find himself confronted with that curious manifestation 'the evening rise', or he will try to cast his fly against a downstream wind, or fish for a carp, or lose a salmon – anyhow he will find out some permanent truths as he goes on, among them the superiority of luck to skill. But it is a sweet madness, *amabilis insanitia* as the poet has said.

H.T. Sheringham, *Ourselves When Young*, 1922.

The Fisherman's Ghost

J.H.R. Bazeley is one of the most unjustly neglected of Edwardian angling writers. His work is always spirited and entertaining: he had a marvellous ear for dialogue and loved stories of mystery and imagination. The following is a good example of his work at its best.

A winter or two after having taken up my permanent abode in the West Riding, I made the necessary arrangements for a couple of days' grayling fishing away up in the dales, as a preparation for the long journey 'home' to the West of England by the midnight express from Leeds on Christmas Eve. Boar Lane, I remember, was soft and slushy from a slight snowfall, and, as I sleepily trudged along to catch the 5 a.m. up north, the atmosphere was chill and moist and laden with the sulphurous fumes from the old steam cars, which were just turning out to give the streets an airing.

On arriving at my destination among the hills, which were clad in virgin white, the crisp snow underfoot, the exhilarating effect of the frosty air, and the pure, clear river, as the ripples danced in the early morning light, were a most delightful change from what I had left behind in smoky Leeds.

F i s h   T a l e s

After a rattling good breakfast at the village coffee taven, and a 'small lemon' with the keeper for luck, I strode out as briskly as waders and brogues would permit towards the succession of streams at the top of the water.

Selecting a shallow run which broke away towards the opposite bank, I sent a little gilt-tail worm along the edge of the fast water, and was rewarded with three good fish in as many swims. It was a full hour before I had finally finished with that fifty yards, and by that time nine or ten beautiful fish lay in the bottom of the basket. Moving to the opposite bank, I spied a couple of young fellows – from Bradford, I learned subsequently – coming round the bend. They were simply amazed to see an angler standing in the water in the depth of winter, and said so pretty bluntly. 'Here, tak' a sup o' this,' said one, as he offered me a fairly commodious bottle, 'you must be frozzen to death.' I thanked him, sampled the contents, and, as the brand was good, did it again. 'Aren't you cold?' he asked, as he took back the lotion. 'Feel that,' I told him, as I put my warm hand into his. 'Well, I'll be danged!' was the comment. 'You must be a bally salamander!'

The good sport continued on every stream I touched, and when the gathering gloom of the short winter's day compelled me to cease fire, thirty-nine lovely grayling, thyme-scented and in the pink of condition, as nearly filled the basket as made no difference. A bee-line was made for the little pub, waders were stripped and turned inside out, and, jolly well tired – for I had been up soon after three – I dropped down into an easy chair in front of a roaring fire in the cosy little parlour, where the vapoury promises of an appetising meal oozed through from the kitchen and reminded me that I had had nothing to eat since noon. I picked up a copy of the old *Daily News*, which proved to be the issue of the previous day, and scanned its stale pages in the genial glow thrown out by the burning logs.

The next morning I made an early start, being determined, if possible, to make a full day of it and fish down the whole of the water. The first stream drew blank, so I rounded the bend to the next. Apparently somebody else had been there before me, for, some distance away, I saw an angler leaving the water to go down below. I followed, and from the stream he had vacated, I did remarkably well. As I began to toddle down to the next pitch the old chap in front of me also made a move, and this continued right through the day. But, judging from the sport I had enjoyed, his presence on the water could have made little or no difference to the number of fish I caught.

I felt decidedly pleased that I should have company for the evening, and when I saw him a few hundred yards in front of me along the little lane leading to our headquarters, I made a spurt to overhaul him. In this, however, I was unsuccessful, and he turned in at the door a short distance ahead.

'Where's the old fellow who's just come in?' I asked the landlord.

'Which one, sir?' he queried.

'Why, the old gentleman who has been fishing,' I replied.

What he said next mildly staggered me.

'You're mista'en, sir, you're the first fisherman we've had in here for over three month.'

'Mistaken? Not much,' I exclaimed. 'Why, I distinctly saw him turn in at the door only a minute or two ago,' and then I proceeded to give a description of the angler who had been dodging me the whole day through.

'Can you spare a minute, sir?' the keeper, who had been an interested listener, whispered to me. I assented, and taking our glasses we retired to the far corner. 'You know the old chap you were talking about, sir? Well, you can tek it from me that you seed 'im reight eniff. He ewsed ter be the only one wot was mad eniff to go ketchin' graylin' all thro' the winter. He hed some narrer squeaks time and time, did t'owd feller, an' was trapped at last in that stream dahn by t'willers. It wor just sich another C'rismas as this 'ere, only there wor 'appen a bit more snow on t'grund. Well, old Bill H – , thet wor 'is name – wor stannin' at t'bottom o' t'stream, when up jumps t'river a foot or two – there'd bin a reight sudden thaw 'ayer up – and tippled poor owd Bill over afore he knowed wheer he wor. We fun 'im fower days efter, tangled up among t'willer roots, an' they ses as ivvery C'rismas Eve he fishes them there same streams an' comes in 'ere to hev a drink just like he used ter dew. But t'boss don't like fresh folk to 'ear abaat it.'

'You'll excuse me bein' a bit rough, sir,' I heard the landlord say quite close to me, 'but yer wor thet fast off – Ah shouted two or three times but yer didn't 'ear – ah hed to give yer a reight good shek.' I could scarcely believe my eyes, for, coming to with a start, there, in front of me, was the same roaring fire,

Perch chasing fry, by A. Rowland Knight

while the table held the substantial sight of the appetising odours previously referred to – a rare good juicy steak with trimmings to match and home-made cheese cakes as a finish off. When I told mine host the theme of my visit to Dreamland his sides shook with honest laughter, and he assured me that I should see 'nowt nowhere nor mesel' on the morrow.

And when the keeper dropped in for a chat shortly afterwards, the subject gave that worthy the opportunity of filling me up with the folklore of the district till midnight arrived, by which time he was pretty well filled up, too.

The second day proved an almost exact replica of the first, for I collected a number of fish identical with the catch of the day before, and had seven prime grayling to take away to my friends in the Test country. But, although I kept a specially keen look-out until the distant hill tops faded to rest in the gathering mists of the winter's afternoon, I got no glimpse of the old chap who was drowned among the willows and who had pottered about in my dreamland swims.

J.H.R. Bazeley, *Fishing Stunts*, 1916.

Fish Tales

The Pike of a Century

In the following extract, Bazeley examines the influence of that which no angler can afford to be without, namely luck.

Two other instances – of the scores I could recall – of the influence of luck may be of interest. Some twenty years ago the owner of a lake – just about twice as large as the top pool at Roundhay – in the West of England, stretched a point and gave me permission to have a day with the pike. The place seemed rather disappointing. There was a big patch of open water in the middle, and another at the top end where a small beck entered, the remainder being completely covered with weeds and reeds. As there was no boat on the lake, I had no option but to fish near the inflow, and from there I quickly got a ten-pounder. Then things became awfully quiet, and for three full hours not a bait was disturbed.

The keeper came round for a chat, but tiring of the monotony of watching a float which refused to bob, at length went his way, after assuring me by all that was holy that there were pike 'in' as big as himself.

Just as the sun was disappearing behind the elms, bang went the float, and never came up again. I let him have thirty seconds, and then gave him a 'oncer'. It was like hitting Yorkshire. He took not the slightest notice, so I did it again, only more so. Then he began to move off towards the reeds, slowly, leisurely, as if he were not in the least bit of a hurry. The heavy rod was bent double, and the line cut my fingers as it passed between them and the butt. And he kept going. I made a great effort to turn him as he neared the reeds, but he kept on and on, and I could see from the commotion in the crackly stems just where he had gone. Then he came to a full stop, and for a full half-hour I pulled and hauled and alternately kept a steady strain, but all to no purpose. He never budged. Thinking he might feel sorry for what he had done, and come back into the open, I gave him a slack line. But with a mighty rush he went twenty yards farther into his weedy fastness, and at length the pressure was relieved by the line snapping several feet above the float, and the pike of a century was gone for ever!

F i s h   T a l e s

Pike takes the bait, by A. Rowland Knight

Only a few weeks afterwards, however, I received a meed of compensation. A friend and I were spinning for salmon on the Wye. I had a run, struck, and, securely hooked, his salmonship made tracks. When he had taken some forty yards from the 'loan office', the line snapped close to the reel like a whip cracking. Later in the day, as we were going down to tea, I discovered my fish – a twenty-pounder – stranded in shallow water, with the line wound round and round him in such a manner as almost to prevent him from making the slightest movement. How or why he had thus trussed himself it is impossible to say. But he had, and saved us from ignominy, for he was the sole catch of the day. So we were again all square.

Far too often, the results of sheer negligence are wrongly ascribed to bad luck. Only the other week, a Leeds angler was grayling fishing on the Yore, and found them in the humour. After catching a score or so, the wrapping of his hook had become seriously damaged, but thinking it would account for 'just one more', he risked it. His float bobbed, he struck, and found he had become moored to a tremendously big chub – anything over six pounds. But five minutes told its tale, the hook drew, and he sighed 'Hard luck'.

'What?' cried the keeper. 'You call it what you like, but if you believe me, it was idleness, and serves you right.' And it did.

J.H.R. Bazeley, *Fishing Stunts*, 1916.

Wasp Hunting

This is one of Bazeley's funniest angling stories. It is as good in its way as Edward Thompson's description in Battles With My Breakfast *of being arrested while hunting lobworms at night on his own lawn.*

The first three nests presented no problem out of the ordinary, and I was very quickly in possession of fifteen or sixteen fine cakes of grub. Nor did the fourth nest – which it was my turn to dig out – appear a particularly difficult proposition, but it is never wise to judge the efficacy of the hair restorer by the picture on the wall. The brown paper was correctly folded and flooded with paraffin, lighted, and introduced into the hole. The turf was then placed in position and a couple of minutes allowed for the complete asphyxiation of the inmates. Then I began digging, and at the third attempt struck the hole. And the wasps struck me and my friend too.

The flame must have failed, for they came out in a cloud. Of course, I dropped the spade and 'bunked' – there is no other word for it – in a hurry. But the wasps were with us, and when we were sufficiently far away to count the spoils, we found that the stings totalled twenty eight, which worked out to five each and three over. And, of course, I had the three over. It was some time before we dared venture back to fetch the spade, and when we did, several of the little friends were still vainly attempting to 'jab' the hard wooden handle with their reverse ends.

Fish Tales

A native sauntered up . . .

We were cowards – arrant cowards – as the circumstance of jointing up the longest rod, tying a loop of string to the top ring, and drawing it gingerly out of the danger zone will plainly indicate. You will probably smile, but then you have never had the pleasure of carrying a few healthy stings about with you. If ever you have, you will also experience the delightful sensation of feeling a wasp crawling up your arm, another down your back, and still another somewhere else. Of course they are only false alarms, but they will keep you busy all the same.

When fishing at Brafferton-on-Swale in the summer of 1905, I was reconnoitring a fairly strong wasp-nest which was built in an overhanging bank a foot or so from the upper level, intending to introduce a little sleep-producer and then complete the operation with a trowel which I always carried for the purpose, when a 'native' sauntered up. He pooh-poohed the idea of an anaesthetic, and as he volunteered to have the thing out in a couple of minutes without any assistance, I stood by for him to do it. After fixing the exact location of the nest, he drew back a couple of paces and then jumped with all his weight on the edge of the bank. The latter gave way – too much so – for as the cakes of grub rolled down the bank he went with them. I don't remember how many stings he got, but he kept his word and collected every cake and brought it to me. He even refused the proffered sixpence, but implored me not to say a word about it at the pub where I was staying. I didn't.

It was during the same season that, returning late on the Thursday night, I left my basket – containing four or five large cakes of grub – and other impedimenta, at the cloak-room, intending to call for it on the following day. Unfortunately, however, a wire was awaiting me calling me away to the South of England, where I was detained for several days. I clean forgot all about my fishing tackle, and it would be a full fortnight before a polite note from the railway company reminded me that it was still at the station.

They had obtained my address from the brass plate on the lid of the basket, and the communication respectfully informed me that if the property were not claimed within seven days the basket would be opened and the contents disposed of at the annual sale to cover the cost of storage! I am afraid I smiled a wicked smile. I wondered how much per thousand tame wasps would fetch at an auction.

When I went down after breakfast my reception at the cloak-room could scarcely be described as cordial. A wasp flew out of the opening to welcome me, and an official squelched another as it alighted on the desk. 'A d – nice thing you've done,' he almost shouted, as I presented the ticket – the number of which he had apparently learned long since – 'making a convenience of the company for housin' a swarm o' bees. You'll 'ear more o' this.' And then he dabbed another.

'Well, you have my name and address,' I said very quietly, 'just give me my property will you?' I thought he was going to have a fit.

'What? – me? – well – I'll be !!! Why, nobody's been able to go near it for three days, and two of the staff's been off – stung in three or four places! That corner's been like a musical box for over a week – here's some more of 'em, look!' And he dodged three or four on their way to the platform. 'No bloomin' fear – not me. If you want your bloomin' bees you come in and fetch 'em, and I hope they'll set about you – right.'

Pulling hard at my pipe, I walked over to the corner indicated, and there were certainly a few wasps about. And I could hear that there were more inside the basket. Losing no time on the way, I dodged round to Miller's and borrowed a large sheet of brown paper in a hurry. In less time than it takes to tell, the basket was securely enveloped and tied up, and then I had time to talk.

On reaching home another problem presented itself, but this was quickly solved. Depositing a saucer of methylated spirit and sulphur in the corner of a packing case in the back yard, applying a lighted match, placing the basket minus the paper in the big box, and popping the lid on. In half an hour's time every wasp was a corpse, and there were hundreds and hundreds of them. Not a single grub was left, and had I only waited another couple of days there would not have been a wasp left either. They would have come out of their temporary home and provided the gentleman at the cloak-room with a little additional diversion. For months and months afterwards, whenever I left my fishing tackle at the station, it was looked upon with suspicion by the people in charge, who invariably propounded the query, 'Onny bees in 'ere, mister?'

J.H.R. Bazeley, *Fishing Stunts*, 1916.

The Four Pounder

Bazeley travelled all over the country in search of good fishing and thought nothing of walking a dozen miles to, and a dozen from, his fishing. Here he recalls a trout fishing foray in the north country.

It was towards the fag end of the Mayfly season – the second Saturday in June, to be correct – that a Leeds expert accompanied me to a little village a few miles from Helmsley on the Rye, our avowed intention being to give the trout a thorough 'plating'.

Unfortunately, the day of our choice turned out a miserable, cold and forbidding affair, just like the yesterday and the day before, and looking in vain for a rise of that most delicately beautiful of all nature's insect efforts – the diaphanous-winged green drake – we descended basely from our proud pedestal and were reduced to catching minnows to use as an alternative lure. For a time the fish were every whit as dour as the day, and gave but a negative indication that they were engaged in the serious occupation of pushing each other out of the way to get at the bait. Then, for some unaccountable reason, they suddenly wakened up and at almost every cast there was a savage little grab.

Five or six nice trout were quickly creeled, and then I found myself at the top of a broad corner. Now this particular spot was specially interesting to me, for the landlord at the little hostelry – where my companion, being an enthusiastic motorist, had persuaded me to call to lubricate the interchangeables – had whispered in my ear that a village expert had been 'broken to blazes' there only the day before by a fish anything up to a yard long, which had retained his fly and a length of gut as a souvenir. I decided, therefore, to spin every inch of it carefully and thoroughly.

The first cast had scarcely been half fished through when there was a decided drag, and I felt that I was at least into something good. Not knowing exactly the strength of the opposition, I gave him his head and allowed him as much latitude – and longitude – as he desired, and in a few minutes slipped the net under – not a yard of trout certainly, but a nice enough fish, which subsequently balanced a pound weight exactly. Well now, I know you'll not believe it; but firmly fixed in its upper jaw was a strawbodied artificial May, with about five inches of gut attached. And such gut! It was of the undrawn grade, and would have made short work of lifting five or six pounds dead weight. Of course, I called to my friend, who was not far away, to witness the proceeding. 'Now,' said he, 'just you lend me that fly and we'll have some fun when we get back to the Bug and Gluepot' – which we did, but more of that anon.

This was to be a day of extraordinaries, apparently, for at the very next cast I hooked something which went off like a streak of lightning and resisted all attempts at breaking for at least twenty yards. I shouted lustily that the other fish was a counterfeit, and that I was securely moored to the 'whopper'. My brother piscator came up at a run to see the fun, and was not disappointed, for

Angling on the River Dart, by J.C. Ibbetson

he put up a rare fight for several minutes, then suddenly caved in and was brought to view – a twelve-ounce fish hooked by the tail! This accounted, of course, for his strenuous but unavailed bid for liberty.

Less than five minutes afterwards two half-pounders actually seized the minnow at one and the same time – the most extraordinary circumstance I have ever heard of in a lifetime of fishing. I was using a small Ariel tackle at the time, and there the little bounders were, one glued to each shoulder triangle. Fortunately for my reputation I was not alone, for my companion saw both fish before they were lifted from the water. Compared with this incident, the surprise occasioned to a swallow on the wing which I accidentally 'bounced' in its flight when making a long cast, and the fact that a hungry trout cleaned the hooks of the minnow and left a worm on the flights in its place are of no account. When that confounded branch cracked off, however, and dropped me into three feet of water, I thought it time to turn it up as things were getting serious; besides, the minnows were all used up.

When we arrived back at headquarters the first person we met was the gent who had lost the 'plugger'. My friend tipped me a wink – what for I did not know – and slid off in a hurry to find mine host. In a minute or two the latter strolled to the door and, addressing the local, intimated that the gentleman inside had caught the fish he had lost the day before. 'Ah shud think he'll be very neer fower,' he observed, and never moved a muscle. 'The devil he will!' was the reply. 'Where is un?'

We went to see, and there on the table, with half-a-dozen grinning yokels grouped around, lay a little troutlet into the mouth of which the rescued fly had been deftly introduced. 'Where's t'fish?' enquired the excited native. 'There,' said the smiling landlord, pointing to the fingerling. 'Ah telled yer 'e wor neerly fower ounces.' Considerable argument ensued, and just as things were getting quite pleasantly warm, the two strangers from Leeds slipped away and reached the station just in time to board the 'slow', en route for the West Riding. But the native got his own back with interest, for the next time we wrote for permission we were politely refused by the owner, and just as politely informed that he objected to permitees retaining small fish!

J.H.R. Bazeley, *Fishing Stunts*, 1916.

On the Trail of the Giant Pike

John Bickerdyke is undoubtedly one of our great angling writers, and this I think is his masterpiece. It has humour, dialogue, pace and the best portrayal of the obsessive angler that I have ever come across.

Now there is nothing remarkable in seeing a rod and reel in Ireland, but these particular weapons made me open my eyes and mouth in amazement. The rod at its point was thick as my little finger, the reel not less than 8 inches in diameter and the line – shades of Izaak Walton! What a line was there. I have towed a canoe up the Thames with cord less thick.

I was on the point of enquiring into the particular uses of this remarkable tackle, when the door of the cabin opened and a short, wiry old man with deep set, piercing eyes, iron-grey hair and clad in a shabby suit of tweeds, came in wearily, bearing just such another rod and reel and a huge basket which I instinctively felt contained fish. He took no notice of me, but gasped out, in a voice which told of his exhausted condition: 'The steelyard, the steelyard!'

With trembling hands he opened the rush basket and turned out of it one of the largest pike I had ever seen. Mrs O'Day who seemed in no way surprised, produced an ancient rusty instrument and proceeded in a businesslike manner to weigh the fish. The old man's excitement while she did this was painful to witness.

'Is it? Is it?' he commenced.

'No, it isn't,' said Mrs O'Day calmly. 'He's 5 lb short.'

I was looking at the fish, but, hearing a groan, turned my eyes to the old fisherman and saw him lying on the floor of the shebeen. He had fainted.

'Poor ould man,' said Mrs O'Day. 'It's disappointed he is and weak too for devil a bit of food has he touched this day since yesterday. Undo his collar sir, and I'll mix him a timperance drink.'

And so her tongue ran on. Meanwhile the old fellow came to himself and sat up, but his eyes went at once to the pike, which still lay on the floor.

'Only 35 lb,' I heard him mutter to himself. 'But I will have him soon. I will have him soon.'

Mrs O'Day's 'timperance' drink was in the nature of an egg flip. It acted like a charm on the old man, who five minutes after drinking it rose, kicked the fish to the side of the cabin and for the first time appeared to be aware that a stranger was in the shebeen. Mrs O'Day noticed the questioning look he cast at me.

'It's a gentleman who lost his way in the bog,' she said.

'Not fishing?' he asked rather anxiously.

'No, snipe shooting,' said I, and he seemed to me greatly relieved at the intelligence. Mrs O'Day now turned out the stew on to a large dish and apologised for having no plates, remarking that she was 'not used to the gentry'. We were both of us more or less famished and talked but little during the meal, after which, Mrs O'Day having provided us with a second edition of the 'timperance' drink, we drew the settle close to the peat fire, and commenced to chat over our pipes.

My new acquaintance, from what I could gather, was an Englishman who had lived for many years in Ireland and apparently passed his whole time in fishing. But I was able to tell him of certain modern methods of pike fishing of which he had heard nothing. By and by he began to get communicative and finally I ventured to ask him why the weighing of the pike had so disturbed him. Without hesitation he told me the following story.

'From a boy . . . I was an enthusiastic fisherman, I need not trouble to tell you how I caught salmon in Norway, gudgeon in the Thames, trout in the Test, and enormous grayling in the Hampshire Avon. I fished whichever and wherever I could and nothing, however large or however small, came amiss to me. But one thing I had never caught – a really large pike. Even in Sweden I never took one over 30 lb. This nettled me, for many were the tales I read of monsters, particularly in the Irish lakes.

'One morning I read in a sporting paper a letter from an Irishman – a tackle dealer so I afterwards ascertained – asking why English anglers did not come more over there. In the lakes in his neighbourhood there was fine pike fishing. Thirty-pounders were common, and they got a forty-pounder or two every season. Here was exactly the information I wanted. I told some friends about it, but they only smiled. I said I would catch a forty- pounder before long. They replied that there was no such thing as a forty-pounder, alive or stufffed. Well, the end of it was I made a bet that I would go to Ireland and before I returned I would catch a fish of that weight.'

I here interrupted his story to tell him of a strange coincidence. It was that very tacklemaker's letter which had first brought me to Ireland. 'But go on,' I said. 'Finish your story and then you shall have mine.'

'I began badly,' he continued, 'I wrote to the man for details of these loughs he mentioned and received a reply from his widow, he having died soon after writing the paragraph. From the poor woman I could get no information. She said she had no idea to which waters her husband referred; in fact, she knew of none. Then I put a letter of enquiry in the sporting papers and received many replies from persons, some of whom were possibly not altogether disinterested in the matter.'

'I have suffered in the same way myself,' I interjected. 'I came to Ireland armed with tackle such as would hold the largest pike that ever lived.' He continued, not noticing my interruption.

'At first I was hopeful. What tales they told me to be sure. There was one of a big pike caught in Lough Derg or, I should say, was killed by some workmen who were digging drains near the lake. The bishop of Killaloo was reputed to be fond of pike, and to him the fish was taken. It was so large that half its body dragged on the ground as two men carried it, slung on a pole, to the bishop's palace. When the bishop saw it, he told them to give it to the pigs. "I am fond of pike," said he, "but distinctly decline to have anything to do with sharks." Ah! What would I not have given to have caught that fish.
'Well, I fished here and I fished there, first trying all the large Shannon Lakes, and then visiting Corrib and Cullen. Thence I went to the north of Ireland, catching now and then some fine fish, but never even a thirty-pounder. The more difficult I found it to attain my object, the more determined I became to succeed. And I shall succeed yet. Let me see. It is now twenty-five years since I came to Ireland. I must have caught thousands of pike in that time – that one there on the floor is the largest of the lot; in fact, the largest I have seen caught by myself or anybody else. This is my second great disappointment. At Athlone I thought I had succeeded. That was a big fish. I took him to the station and weighed him there. 'Forty-three pounds,' said the station master.
'A Major Brown who was looking on began to prod the fish with his stick. "Something hard there", he said. "Let's cut him open and see what he had for dinner."
'I would not agree to this as I wanted the skin entire, but the major squeezed him a bit and up came a lot of swan shot which my scoundrel of a

boatman had evidently poured down his throat so that he might earn the reward I had promised him if I caught a heavy fish.

'But at last I really have found a monster pike – the catching of him is only a question of time. Not a quarter of a mile from this cabin [here he lowered his voice to a whisper] is a deep reedy lake. The priest has a boat on it, which he lends me. I was rowing along the other evening when something struck the boat with such force that I was thrown from the seat and nearly capsized. It was in deep water and there are no rocks in the lake. I had rowed right on to a pike as large as a calf.'

He said the last sentence slowly and earnestly. I expect I showed great interest in the statement for, like the old man, it had long been my ambition to catch a really immense pike.

'Well,' said I, 'let us go and try the lake together. I should like to help you land such a monster.'

'Ah, but you might catch him and not I. How then?' And he gave me a very unpleasant look out of his deep-set eyes.

We said nothing for a while, when my companion suddenly startled me by asking if I was aware that he was the Emperor of Germany. I said I was not, and another unpleasant silence ensued.

Mrs O'Day had made up two heather beds for us on the mud floor and without undressing we each stretched ourselves on our moorland couches.

Just as I was dropping off to sleep, my companion got up on his elbow and said gravely: 'Hang me if I don't believe you are a pike. I'll have a triangle into you tomorrow morning. Good night.'

There was no doubt about it. He was mad. I dared not go to sleep. I made a pretence of it until the old man began to snore and then sat by the fire until daybreak when, leaving some money on the table for Mrs O'Day, I sped away over the moor.

Years afterwards I was telling the tale of the demented angler who, I felt certain, had lost his wits in his unavailing search after a big Irish pike, when I was interrupted by Rooney, of the Irish Bar, who burst into a peal of laughter, swearing that he knew my pike-fishing acquaintance well and that there was no saner man in Ireland.

'Fact is Johnny,' said he, 'the old boy was fearful you would get that big fish before him and so he thought he would frighten you home.'

Rooney may say what he likes, but I decline to believe in the sanity of any man who expatriates himself during a quarter of a century in the endeavour to catch a 40 lb pike.

John Bickerdyke, *Wild Sport in Ireland*, 1895.

A Pike on the Attack

This short but fascinating extract, written anonymously by a newspaper reporter of the day, is one of the very few credible instances of a freshwater fish attacking a human.

One of my sons, aged fifteen, went with three other boys to bathe in Inglemere Pond, near Ascot racecourse. He walked gently into the water to about the depth of 4 ft when he spread out his hands to attempt to swim. Instantly a large fish came up and took his hand into his mouth as far up as the wrist, but, finding he could now swallow it, relinquished his hold, and the boy, turning round, prepared for a hasty retreat out of the pond, his companions, who saw it, also scrambled out of the pond as fast as possible.

My son had scarcely turned himself round when the fish came up behind and immediately seized his other hand crosswise, inflicting some very deep wounds on the back of it. The boy raised his first-bitten and still bleeding arm, and struck the monster a hard blow on the head, then the fish disappeared.

The other boys assisted him to dress, bound up his hand with their handker-chiefs, and brought him home. We took him down to Mr Brown, surgeon, who dressed seven wounds in one hand; and so great was the pain the next day, that the lad fainted twice; the little finger was bitten through the nail and it was more than six weeks before it was well. The nail came off and the scar remains to this day.

Reading Mercury, June 1856.

This anonymous woodcut from the mid-seventeenth century
is one of the earliest surviving angling illustrations

An Infallible Anointment for Fish Bait

Anyone who thinks that modern carp baits are becoming ridiculously contrived and complicated will be fascinated by the following extract, which explains how our French cousins sorted out their bait problems a few hundred years ago.

Take of man's fat and cat's fat, of each half an ounce; mummy, finely powdered, three drams; cumium seed, finely powdered, one dram; distilled oil of aniseed and spike, of each six drops; civet, two grains; and campline, four grains; make an ointment according to art.

When you angle with this, anoint 8 in of line next the hook. Keep it in a pewter box, made something taper; and when you use it never angle with less than two or three hairs next the hook because if you do and angle with one hair, it will not stick well to the line.

Recommended by M. Charras to Louis XIV, King of France.

Fish Tales

Seeing Eye to Eye

A gruesome little tale this, but one which suggests that fish are not quite as sensitive as some would have us believe.

A very singular, though I believe not unparalleled instance of the voracity of the perch occurred to me while fishing in Windermere. In removing the hook from the jaws of the fish, one eye was accidentally displaced and remained adhering to it. Knowing the reparative capabilities of piscine organisation, I returned the maimed perch, which was too small for my basket, to the lake, and, being somewhat scant of minnows, threw the line in again with the eye attached as bait – there being no other of any description on the hook.

The float disappeared almost instantly and on landing the newcomer, it turned out to be the fish I had the moment before thrown in, and which had thus been actually caught on his own eye.

H. Cholmondely Pennell, *Perch Fishing*, 1886.

The Stranger on the Shore

Here sea angling is central to a curious little piece of fiction by a writer now almost totally forgotten. The atmosphere and mystery of a lonely windswept sea shore is nowhere better expressed.

We fished for years, my Uncle and I, down where the sea met the river and such was the remoteness of the place that never once did we see another man or child crossing the wide flat sands of the estuary. Never, that is, until one year's end long ago.

We had spent the day repairing the house which stood alone, bleached and whitened by centuries of wind and salt. Even the furniture was centuries old by then, it was as old as the house and each piece so heavy and crooked, but each piece a part of our lives.

F i s h   T a l e s

So we had spent that day repairing the weatherboarding with odd planks that we found washed up on the beach. They made the house look more ramshackle year by year, but since no one else ever saw it what did that matter? When occasionally we stopped to exchange a few words we automatically looked out over the distant waters in case a ship was passing. But it was years since anything had passed this way.

Then, in the early afternoon, Uncle suggested that we try fishing. It was a bad day for it, too cold and the wind all wrong, but I didn't like to argue with Uncle. We took out the heavy rods and the great brass reels and tramped down to the water's edge. Uncle could cast beautifully and though I watched him for many years I never really learned the art. He threw our lines eighty, perhaps one hundred yards out into the low, angry surf, and then we waited.

The thick cane rod tops nodded gently towards the water keeping time with the movement of the waves, but no fish disturbed their rhythm. As usual, we watched out to sea, saying nothing to each other because long silences were our way. If we had spent some time watching back over the flat lands behind us we might have seen the stranger coming. But it would have made no difference. We would have stayed and waited for him because there was nothing else to do.

'Anything doing?'

The voice behind us, not startling, but strong and confident. The owner of the voice wore an old, greasy jersey over his head in the strangest fashion.

The ends of the two sleeves were tied with string and a drawstring had been fitted to the waist. The jersey had then been stuffed with newspaper, the two thickly filled sleeves tied under the man's chin, the body of the garment riding fat and high above his head. The rest of his clothes appeared to be made from a million layers of rags and scarves and tatters of old coats and jackets. He was almost emaciated, to judge by his face, but he wore so many layers of clothing that he looked like a giant. Uncle and I only stared at him.

'Anything doing?' he said again. 'Perhaps it's not such a good day for fishing. Perhaps you should be home by the fire, with the doors locked against the wind.'

Then, looking at me, he said: 'Try casting that bit closer into the gullies where the poor fish lie to escape the coldest waves.'

F i s h T a l e s

'We don't know you,' my Uncle almost shouted. He looked at the stranger with undisguised ill-feeling, then he turned and faced back out to sea.

'Your uncle won't take an old man's advice,' said the stranger to me.

Not knowing what to say in reply, I said nothing, but I knew something had made Uncle angry. When I reeled in to check my hooks I couldn't resist trying a short cast into the foam; it suited me since I could never hope to compete with a champion caster like my Uncle. Almost as soon as my bait hit the water I caught a fat cod and then another and another.

The stranger watched with a calm face, saying nothing, but all the while watching Uncle's back. Soon I had a basketful of fish, but I couldn't bring myself to thank the stranger in front of my Uncle, who all the while had stayed silent and kept his face to the sea.

Evening was coming in and still we three stood on the edge of the sea as if we were the only people in the world. Then, without a word, Uncle lifted his great rod and reeled in. He had caught nothing. As we packed away our things, the stranger came closer and asked if we would give him a fish. I looked at Uncle, wondering what I should do. He took no notice and packed our fish into his bag.

'Would you give me a fish?' said the stranger once again, but this time directly to my Uncle who, suddenly and without a word, struck the man hard across the face. He fell and as he lay there my Uncle pushed me past him, across the sands and back towards the house.

That night we ate the cod and listened in silence to the wind. In the morning, my Uncle was dead.

Robert Green, *Tales of the Sea*, 1890.

A Trout on a Pea-Shooter

Craft and guile are vitally important in fishing (and in making sure one wins one's wager), as the following delightful piece from the pen of the great John Bickerdyke reveals.

He was an old and wise fish, and had his headquarters opposite a clubhouse on a certain famous stream. Many a fly had passed over his venerable head. Once long ago it is said that he was hooked on a piece of bread, but quickly wound the line round a stump, extracted the hook and was rising to some natural flies half an hour later. New members used to bet that they would catch him. The old members took their bets and their money and obtained satisfaction out of the fish that way. It was an aggravating feature in that trout's behaviour that nothing would put him down short of a cart rope thrown over his head. He was as tame as a pug dog, but had the cunning, without the wildness, of a hawk.

One day there joined the club a man who was not an expert with the fly rod. He, like the rest, said he thought he could catch the trout. The old members laughed and took his bets, as was their custom with newcomers. A mean thing this, but very much the way of the world.

It was August. One sultry evening the new member came to the club armed with a pea-shooter and many bluebottles. Was he going to catch the trout with a pea-shooter? No; he was only going to begin to catch him – the operation might take some time. Deftly a half-dead bluebottle was puffed out of the tube in front of the fish. It was taken, of course, as everything eatable from a trout's point of view was taken. The fish had a rare supper that evening.

The following day the new member repeated the operation. He fed the fish in this manner for more than a week; the others smiled and looked on.

'I will catch him soon,' said the new member. 'I am only waiting for wind.'

At the end of three weeks there came a day when a stiff breeze was blowing upstream. It was the day on which the catastrophe was fated to happen. The new member appeared at the clubhouse with a long slender rod, on which was arranged running tackle and a length of fine, but strong gut, terminating with a single hook.

Deep wading. An illustration by the nineteenth-century amateur artist, Joseph Crawhall

He took his stand some distance below the fish, and began feeding him as usual. On the hook was a bluebottle. Good luck helped our friend who, however, exhibited considerable skill. The upstream breeze took the hooked fly just over the trout, and the new member let it fall and at the same time puffed out a fly from the tube.

Which would the trout take? It was an anxious moment. Had the rod been in front instead of behind him, he would have taken neither. But he did not see the rod, having no eyes in his tail (this has been questioned) and the fly containing the hook was sucked in.

How he fought! Was the wisdom of twenty years to culminate in destruction by means of a pea-shooter and a bluebottle? Where was that invaluable stump? The new member had removed it. The weeds? They had been recently cut. A leap for liberty then? That made matters worse for the gut got wound round his body and hampered him sadly. But let fall the curtain. He died – as wise and grand and noble a specimen as has ever been seen in a trout stream.

John Bickerdyke, *Days of My Life*, 1895.

Fly Fishing the Sea

Few practise the gentle art of fly fishing on the high seas today, but our Victorian ancestors were not so timorous, as the following delightful extract shows.

Never on salmon river or trout stream have I enjoyed more splendid fly fishing than has fallen to my lot from Filey Brigg. Sometimes so eager were the fish that if one missed the fly another was hooked immediately afterwards. It was simply a fight against time and a rising tide.

The enthusiastic sea-fisher may claim for the sea the first place in the variety of sport afforded, but he must admit that, on its literary side it is a very bad second in its rivalry with river and lake.

From the time of Izaak Walton, freshwater fishing has been the subject of a series of most charming works, some of them, in parts, almost prose poems. And a fascination, I may say glamour, has been cast over trout, salmon and other fish which will remain until English angling literature is forgotten.

Sea fish and sea fishing, notwithstanding their national importance, have a very small niche indeed in our literature, probably because until the middle of this century, the coarseness of the tackle commonly used deterred most anglers, so many of whom are men of refined literary tastes.

John Bickerdyke, *Sea Fishing*, 1895.

Fish Tales

Never on a Sunday

This story has a decidedly apocryphal aura about it, but it is a wonderful example of the classic gillie anecdote.

Two anglers – both Sassenachs – had waited at Loch Awe for a breeze for a whole week and waited in vain. On the sabbath morn there was a glorious ripple; the kind of ripple in which a trout rushes madly at the angler's fly. Fish those anglers must. The gillie was an elder of the kirk and he turned up the whites of his eyes when they suggested he should just let them have the boat for an hour or two.

'I could nae do it, such a thing has no been done on the loch within the memory of man.'

They offered untold bribes of silver and gold, but the gillie was obdurate, until his eyes rested on the gold sovereign held out to him.

'Nae, nae,' he said. 'I'll nae let the boat. I'm an elder of the kirk ye ken, and a God-fearing man and it's no reasonable to expect me to consent to such a wicked proceeding, but the boat lies there in the rushes and the oars are in her. Just ye gang away doon and get in her and row awa oot the lake and I'll come doon and swear at ye, but ye must take no notice of what I say. Just row away and I'll call for the money the morn.'

The Angler, 1899.

Giants of the Stein

Abel Chapman, who was best known as a wildfowler, here recalls the loss of not one but two very big Norwegian salmon.

It was a Sunday evening. As the end of the week drew near we had been anxious as to local customs with regard to Sunday fishing – these varying in different parts of Norway. Erik had told us we might fish after dinner; and Gjertrud, our laughter-loving handmaiden who happily seemed to find something comical in almost everything we said and did, propounded the brilliant idea. 'Yes, but you can dine at ten and begin fishing at eleven o'clock.' There was subtlety about this capable of infinite development, but it struck us as too refined, so we delayed starting until four in the afternoon; the greater population of the village, we observed, accompanying our *stolkjaer* or making short cuts through the woods.

When I commenced to cast Stein Pool from the platform, there was an audience of thirty-four folks, lads and lassies, old men and maidens, assembled on the bank behind.

Stein Pool is dead and deep, with a moderate stream running in beyond midriver, and the fish lying well in towards the opposite bank, which was heavily wooded down to the brink. The nearer half of the river is (in fine water) a deep black set where the line, if allowed to enter, is instantly drowned. This combination necessitates not only long casting, but rapid long throws and quick returns, which means hard work, especially as a high bank, twenty yards behind, involved lifting the line well up in the air. The swish of the line in the faces of the spectators soon cleared them off to safer distances, and about halfway down the pool there came that tug – no, it is not a tug, but a sudden inflexible resistance as of a tree trunk or solid rock. But I knew that a big fish had annexed the fly, deep under and without showing, and delayed not to drive the small double hook well home into his jaws.

Five minutes later, after a prolonged period of bottom fighting, jagging and sulking, alternated with sub-aquatic gymnastics and contortions that kept me trembling for my tackle the captive came up with a sudden rush to the surface, ploughing along on his bent broadside for twenty yards. Then we saw that this fish was even bigger than the lost monster of Samkomme. Was it possible to subdue such a salmon on that paltry hook? True, it was double, that reflection seemed inspiring. But then the hooks were smaller than that which had already failed, being actually the smallest (No. 5) in all my collection and therefore specially selected for fine water in a streamless pool.

I determined rightly or wrongly to play for safety, to act solely on the defensive, and to leave the fish to kill himself, even though it involved my spending the night with him in the process.

I pass over details which would involve repetition. Suffice it that the fish, persistently dropping downstream, obliged me to follow. This for some distance was easy enough, but lower down trees grew to the water's edge. Still it was necessary to follow, having some fifty yards of line out. The fish was now in the shallows, rolling heavily at intervals with short, sullen rushes during one of which I felt a slight 'draw' – perhaps the hold of one hook had failed.

W. going down through the trees to reconnoitre reported the fish tired. For almost minutes at a time he lay inert in midstream, suffering himself to be towed ahead in the slack pool-tail without resistance. Had it now been possible to incline the rod inland an opportunity to gaff might, it seemed probable, be secured. But the thickset branches projecting far across the stream forbade this and two alternatives remained. One was to drop still lower downstream trusting to find shallows and get in the cleek at the foot of the pool.

This, however, I rejected, first, because the fish was yet in no sense under control and the danger in the stronger stream obvious, nor was there any reasonable certainty of gaffing there. Secondly, because I knew nothing of the depth or nature of the water below, beyond seeing that there was a strong rapid at least two hundred yards long with an island in midstream and thick wood on either bank. Hence I elected the other course, and endeavoured slowly to tow the half-beaten fish upstream and thus clear the trees. A stone thrown in below the fish's tail at this point might have served the purpose, but we did not think of it at the time.

While thus engaged, though exerting no special pressure – indeed, humouring the captive in all his little runs and lunges – the rod flew up and the fly came home unharmed. The fight was over and the fish the victor.

A few days after in the Stein Pool, I hooked another monster. I felt him come, struck at the right moment, yet in rather less than a minute, for some reason unexplained, the hook came away. During his short captivity he had made one long surface run thus showing up his size.

The conclusions we came to were these. That these very heavy fish given the best of holds on single gut may take an hour to land and possibly more, and that during so prolonged a pressure the hold of a small hook (in fine water no other is of any use) must almost necessarily wear itself out.

I give for what it may be worth, the quality and rank of the two above named fish, these points being set down by estimate by the local experts.

1. The Samkomme fish, forty pounds, fresh from sea the night before.

2. The Stein Pool fish, a larger salmon, probably from forty to fifty, but of some fourteen days sojourn in the river.

These estimates I take to be fairly near the mark. After landing heavy fish one comes to know the strength and style of the twenty-pounder and of fish ranging between that and thirty pounds.

There are old hands among anglers who never fail to land a fish. They may smile at this record of disaster, pointing out things done that should have been avoided, or neglected that should have been tried. Well, to criticise is easy; so, too, is it to haul out heavy but ill-conditioned autumn fish from the depths of some sluggish hole. But with fresh-run springers in Scandinavian streams the case is different and the difficulty greater and more varied.

Abel Chapman, *Wild Norway, 1897.*

A Giant from the Thames

The great Victorian angler Frederic Halford here recalls the capture of that now almost extinct species, the Thames trout.

The usual feeding ground of the big trout was in the blackwater between two runs, just above the lower bay of the weir, and a bright bleak about five inches in length having been deftly arranged so as to spin truly on the flight, I took up my place in the punt. Rosewell [his man] meanwhile, was mounted on the beam of the weir prospecting about with live dace, on the chance of coming across another prowling fish. I proceeded to spin steadily backwards and forwards and up and down the two runs and the intervening wedge of black water, and just as a distant church clock struck seven o'clock, as I was drawing my bait up to the apron of the weir, a number of small fry flew in all directions, and a rush through the water indicated the presence of the fish we were trying

The moment of truth. An anonymous copperplate illustration from about 1780

for. I let my bait gently down, and was drawing it across the stream, when a faint tap made me imagine that a perch or a chub had run at it.

In far less time than it has taken to read these words I struck firmly, my reel was flying round, and a heavy fish plunged at a great rate right down and through the broken white water of the run. It took about forty yards of line in this rush, and then jumped into the air, showing us the outline of a noble trout.

The fish then bored deep in the water and tore across the runs towards the upper end of the weir. Meanwhile, Rosewell, who had, of course, seen what had occurred, stepped into the punt and quietly worked it along the weir to the bay at the lower end, and then to the bank. I got out, and steadying the fish, found it close under the piles of the weir.

On the bank there stood a tree just at the lower end of the weir and I had to lower my rod to pass it round. As I did this the trout made a rush towards me, and although I gathered in the line by hand as rapidly as possible, there was a good deal of slack. To my horror, on recovering this, I found that the line was foul of a willow which grew in the angle of the bay. The position was a desperate one, but Rosewell proved equal to the occasion. Landing net in hand, he stepped into the water and walked down the slippery slope, over which a strong stream was flowing. I trembled, imagining that he intended to try to net the fish, but his judgment was too good for that. Steadying himself with the handle of the landing net, he took out his knife, opened it, and stooping down, cut away the part of the willow round which the line was foul. As it came clear I raised my rod, and obtaining a good pull at the fish, it started across the weir, and again flung itself into the air.

The rest was easy, the trout kept boring down and plunging heavily, while at every favourable opportunity I reeled in and presented the butt. At last the plucky fish came to the surface, and just as it rolled over on its side the sun peeped out of the clouds and revealed to our eyes as fair a sight as ever appeared to a fisherman.

In a very few moments it was in the net and on the bank and both Rosewell and I fairly fell upon it for fear of its jumping back into the water. A more perfect specimen of a Thames trout I never saw, although I certainly have seen larger ones.

Before Rosewell extracted the hook from the mouth we made an examination of the manner in which the fish was hooked. It may have been purely accidental, or it may have pointed the efficacy of hanging the triangle on the reverse side of the bait. But this had embedded itself deeply in the side of the mouth and the other triangles were all hanging loose.

At this moment the local angler came through the lock in his punt and joined us at the side of the weir. He was naturally sorrowful at our being on the spot before him, but he, in true sportsmanlike spirit, conveyed his warmest congratulations, and insisted on us sampling a curious home-made liquor to drink the health of all good fishermen. After a brief consultation I decided to take the trout down to Halliford in the canoe and get it accurately weighed. On my arrival at the Ship Hotel the landlord put it into the scales and it registered $9\frac{3}{4}$ lb. As it was the largest I had hooked and landed, it was despatched to London the same day, and the work of setting it up in a case entrusted to, and most admirably carried out by, Cooper.

This was my last Thames trout, and as the time went on the attractions of fly fishing, and especially dry fly fishing, gradually impelled me to drop all other forms of sport to follow that which may fairly be described as more scientific and more engrossing than any other.

F.M. Halford, *An Angler's Autobiography*, 1903.

Sheringham's Carp

No one has bettered the following description of battling with a big carp. It was written in 1913 by H.T. Sheringham.

For practical purposes there are big carp and small carp. The latter you may sometimes hope to catch without too great a strain on your capabilities. The former – well, men *have* been known to catch them, and there are just a few anglers who have caught a good many. I myself have caught one, and I will make bold to repeat the tale of the adventure as it was told in *The Field* of July 1, 1911.

The narrative contains most of what I know concerning the capture of big carp. The most important thing in it is the value which it shows to reside in a modicum of good luck.

So far as my experience goes, it is certain that good luck is the most vital part of the equipment of him who would seek to slay big carp . . .

And so to my story. I had intended to begin it in a much more subtle fashion, and only by slow degrees to divulge the purport of it, delaying the finale as long as possible, until it should burst upon a bewildered world like the last crashing bars of the 1812 Overture.

Now that a considerable section of the daily press has taken cognisance of the event, it is no good my delaying the modest confession that I have caught a large carp. It is true. But it is a slight exaggeration to state that the said carp was decorated with a golden ring bearing the words, '*Me valde dilexit atque ornavit propter immensitatem meam Issachius Walton, anno Domini MD CIII.*'

Fish Tales

Nor was it the weightiest carp ever taken. Nor was it the weightiest carp of the present season. Nor was it the weightiest carp of June 24. Nor did I deserve it. But enough of negation. Let me to the story which will explain the whole of it.

To begin with, I very nearly did not go at all because it rained furiously most of the morning. To continue, towards noon the face of the heavens showed signs of clearness and my mind swiftly made itself up that I would go after all. I carefully disentangled the sturdy rod and the strong line, the triangle hooks, and the other matters which had been prepared the evening before, and started armed with roach tackle. The loss of half a day had told me that it was vain to think of big carp. You cannot of course fish for big carp in half a day. It takes a month.

I mention these things by way of explaining why I had never before caught a really big carp, and also why I do not deserve one now. As I have said, I took with me to Cheshunt Lower Reservoir roach tackle, a tin of small worms, and intention to try for perch, with just a faint hope of tench. The natural condition of the water is weed, the accumulated growth of long years. When I visited it for the first time some eight years ago I could see nothing but weed, and that was in midwinter. Now, however, the Highbury Anglers, who have rented the reservoir, have done wonders towards making it fishable.

A good part of the upper end is clear, and elsewhere there are pitches cut out which make excellent feeding grounds for fish and angling grounds for men. Prospecting I soon came to the forked sticks, which have a satisfying significance to the ground-baitless angler. Someone else had been there before, and the newcomer may perchance reap the benefit of another man's sowing. So I sat me down on an empty box thoughtfully and began to angle. It is curious how great, in enclosed water especially, is the affinity between small worms and small perch. For two hours I struggled to teach a shoal of small perch that hooks pull them distressfully out of the water.

It was in vain. Walton must have based his 'wicked of the world' illustration on the ways of small perch.

I had returned about twenty and was gloomily observing my float begin to bob again when a cheery voice, that of Mr R.G. Woodruff, behind me, observed that I ought to catch something in that swim. I had certainly fulfilled the obligations and it dawned on me that he was not speaking of small perch and then that my rod was resting on the forked stick and myself on the wooden box of the Hon. Secretary of the Anglers' Association. He almost used force to make me stay where I was, but who was I to occupy a place so carefully baited for carp, and what were my insufficient rod and flimsy line that they should offer battle to 10-pounders? Besides, there was tea waiting for me, and I had had enough of small perch.

So I made way for the rightful owner of the pitch, but not before he had given me a good store of big lobworms, also earnest advice to try for carp with them, roach rod or no roach rod. He told me of a terrible battle of the evening before when a monster took his worm in the dark and also his cast and hook. Whether it travelled north or south he could hardly tell in the gloom but it travelled far and successfully. He hoped that after the rain there might be a chance of a fish that evening.

Finally, I was so far persuaded that during tea I looked out a strong cast and a perch hook on fairly stout gut, and soaked them in the teapot till they were stained a light brown. Then, acquiring a loaf of bread by good fortune, I set out to fish. There were plenty of other forked sticks here and there which showed where other members had been fishing, and I finally decided on a pitch at the lower end, which I remembered from the winter as having been the scene of an encounter with a biggish pike that got off after a considerable fight.

There, with a background of trees and bushes, some of whose branches made handling a 14 foot rod rather difficult, it is possible to sit quietly and fairly inconspicuous. And there accordingly I sat for three hours and a quarter, watching a float which only moved two or three times when a small perch pulled the tail of the lobworm, and occupying myself otherwise by making pellets of paste and throwing them out as ground bait.

Though fine it was a decidedly cold evening, with a high wind; but this hardly affected the water, which is entirely surrounded by a high bank and a belt of trees. Nor was there much to occupy the attention except when some great fish would roll over in the weeds far out, obviously one of the big carp, but a hundred yards away. An occasional moorhen and a few rings made by small roach were the only signs of life. The black tip of my float about eight yards away, in the dearth of other interests began to have an almost hypnotising

influence. A little after half past eight this tip trembled and then disappeared
and so intent was I on looking at it that my first thought was a mild wonder as
to why it did that. Then the coiled line began to go through the rings, and I
realised that there was a bite. Rod in hand, I waited until the line drew taut,
and struck gently. Then things became confused. It was as though some sub-
marine suddenly shot out into the lake. The water was about six feet deep, and
the fish must have been near the bottom, but he made a most impressive wave
as he dashed straight into the weeds about twenty yards away and buried himself in them. And so home, I murmured to myself, or words to that effect for I
saw not the slightest chance of getting a big fish out with a roach rod and fine
line. After a little thought, I decided to try handlining, as one does for trout,
and getting hold of the line – with some difficulty because the trees prevented
the rod point going far back – I proceeded to feel for the fish with my hand.

At first there was no response; the anchorage seemed immovable. Then I
thrilled to a movement at the other end of the line which gradually increased
until the fish was on the run again, pushing the weeds aside as he went, but
carrying a great streamer or two with him on the line. His run ended, as had
the first, in another weed patch, and twice after he seemed to have found safety
in the same way. Yet each time handlining was efficacious, and eventually I got
him into the strip of clear water; here the fight was an easier affair, though by
no means won. It took, I suppose, some fifteen or twenty minutes before I saw a
big bronze side turn over, and was able to get about half the fish into my
absurdly small net. Luckily by this time he had no fight left in him, and I
dragged him safely up the bank and fell upon him. What he weighed I had no
idea, but I put him at about twelve pounds, with a humble hope that he might
be more.

At any rate, he had made a fight that would have been considered very fair in
a twelve-pound salmon, the power of his runs being certainly no less and the
pace of them quite as great. On the tackle I was using, however, a salmon
would have fought longer.

The fish knocked on the head, I was satisfied, packed up my tackle, and went
off to see what the other angler had done. So far he had not had a bite, but he
meant to go on as long as he could see, and hoped to meet me at the train. He
did not do so, for a very good reason; he was at that moment engaged in a grim

battle in the darkness with a fish that proved ultimately to be one ounce heavier than mine, which, weighed on the scales at the keeper's cottage, was sixteen pounds five ounces.

As I owe him my fish, because it was his advice that I put on the strong cast, and the bait was one of his lobworms, he might fairly claim the brace. And he would deserve them, because he is a real carp fisher and has taken great pains to bring about his success. For myself — well, luck attends the undeserving now and then. One of them has the grace to be thankful.

H.T. Sheringham, *Coarse Fishing*, 1913.

A Barbel on a Single Hair

Francis Francis was a prodigiously skilled fisherman who wrote beautifully about tackle, techniques and the atmosphere of fishing. Here he describes a remarkable battle with a big barbel he hooked on a particularly frail line.

Fishing for barbel with fine roach tackle is certainly productive of the most sport, though it is not the way to make a large bag; for, if the angler be using fine roach tackle and hooks a good fish, he may waste an hour and a half over him, and then lose him after all, as I have done scores of times.

I always fished with a single hair formerly, when float fishing from a punt, and have killed very many barbel of four and five pounds weight with it; but so much time and so many fish were lost at it that I have long discontinued it.

I once remember, many years since, hooking an apparently large fish on a single hair, about five o'clock one November afternoon. I played him for a long time until my arm grew tired, when I handed the rod to a friend who was with me. He tired and gave the rod to Wisdom, who in turn, gave it back to me. They both despaired of ever killing the fish and set his weight at a dozen pounds at least. 'He'll take you all night, sir,' said Wisdom.

'Then I'll stop with him all night if he does not break me, for I never have been able to kill one of these big ones with a single hair,' was my reply.

I had often on the same spot hooked three or four of these monsters in a morning, but I never could kill one of them. They always got away, for not far below us was a large deep hole, full of snags, old roots, and rubbish; and sooner or later they always remembered their hole there, and dashed into it headlong. Even stout ledger tackle would hardly have held them and that they were very shy at, preferring the single hair greatly. This hole was about fifty yards below us, and I constantly expected the fish would make for it. However, though he made constant runs, he never cared to go above half the distance, but sheered about, now out in the stream, and now in towards the bank.

It had long been dark, and he showed no symptoms of tiring, though he had in turn tired all of us. Playing a fish in the dark is awkward work, so we hailed some men, several of whom, attracted by the report of our having hooked 'a big 'un', were standing on the bank, to bring us a couple of lanthorns and some hot brandy and water for it was bitterly cold; and with the aid of the lanthorns we at length managed to get the net under the fish and lifted him out. It was half past eight when he was landed, so that I had him on three and half hours. And now what does the reader think he weighed?

Fish Tales

I was disgusted to find that he was only a six-and-a-half pound fish; had I known it I would have broken from him hours before; but it turned out that he was hooked by the back fin, and his head being perfectly free, he of course played as heavily as a fish of double the size; and even now, remembering what the stream was, I wonder how I did succeed in landing him, as a fish so hooked, having his broadside opposed to the water, has great powers of resistance. Indeed I consider that the accomplishment was equal to killing a fish of double the weight if properly hooked.

The feat may sound incredible – three and a half hours with only a single horse hair, a fin-hooked fish, and a heavy stream – nevertheless it is strictly true. Had the hold been in the mouth instead of the hard tough fin, it would probably have cut out half the time.

Francis Francis, *A Book on Angling*, 1896.